Praise for *The Blueprint for My Girls*

"Yasmin Shiraz answers the questions the way that we all wish we could have had them answered for us when we were growing up. *Blueprint* is strong and direct and yet sprinkled with all of the nurturing and love that can inspire these young women to discover and develop their beauty— inside and out."

—BET.com

"Yasmin Shiraz has written an excellent book filled with everyday wisdom and commonsense advice. Although this book would be great for any woman to read, it is a must for teenagers and young adults. After you're finished reading *The Blueprint for My Girls*, you will be amazed how much wisdom is packed into such a short book."

—*Right On!* magazine

"[*The Blueprint for My Girls*] informs, motivates, inspires, and comforts."

—*BlackGirl Magazine*

"*The Blueprint for My Girls* is an inspirational book that does exactly what it promises: shows the reader how to become the woman she aspires to be. Shiraz challenges the reader to ask herself hard questions and change her life accordingly. What I loved most is that it demands that the reader take responsibility for her life but it is communicated in a kind and embracing manner."

—Rosalind Wiseman, author of *Queen Bees & Wannabes*

"Shiraz's book of 99 affirmations does get essential points across. *Blueprint* provides many springboards for self-exploration."

—Rebecca Louie, *Daily News*

"Yasmin Shiraz coaches girls and sets them off on the road leading to strong women who navigate life on their own terms. Offering firsthand experience and proactive advice on how to ride out life's bumps and surprises, her book points the way to an empowered life full of courage, determination, and self-love."

—Erzsi Deàk, editor of *Period Pieces*

"Yasmin has put together this easy-to-read book that girls can keep handy as they make critical choices and shape their futures."

—Catherine Dee, author of *The Girls' Book of Success* and *The Girls' Book of Wisdom*

"While this book is targeted at young females, some of the lessons might also ring true for the mature woman. *The Blueprint for My Girls* is one of those books that can enlighten those of us who believe that we have learned all there is to learn about life."

—DallasBlack.com

"I recommend this book to girls of all ages. It's a useful road map for things women usually have to learn the hard way . . . by making mistakes."

—Olivia, singer/songwriter

the BLUEPRINT for my *Girls*

How to Build a Life Full of Courage, Determination, & Self-love

YASMIN SHIRAZ

A FIRESIDE BOOK
Published by Simon & Schuster
New York   London   Toronto   Sydney

FIRESIDE
Rockefeller Center
1230 Avenue of the Americas
New York, NY 10020

First Fireside Edition 2004

FIRESIDE and colophon are registered trademarks
of Simon & Schuster, Inc.

For information regarding special discounts for bulk purchases,
please contact Simon & Schuster Special Sales at 1-800-456-6798
or business@simonandschuster.com

Designed by Jaime Putorti

Manufactured in the United States of America

10   9   8   7   6   5   4   3   2   1

Library of Congress Cataloging-in-Publication Data
Shiraz, Yasmin.
    The blueprint for my girls : how to build a life full of courage,
    determination, & self-love / Yasmin Shiraz.—1st Fireside ed.
        p.   cm.
    "A Fireside book."
    1. Teenage girls—Psychology. 2. Teenage girls—Conduct of life.
    3. Young women—Psychology. 4. Young women—Conduct of life.
    5. Self-perception in adolescence. 6. Self-esteem in adolescence.
    7. African American teenage girls—Psychology. I. Title.
    HQ798 .S468 2004   305.235'2—dc22   2003059199

ISBN 978-0-7432-5214-0
ISBN 0-7432-5214-4

This book is dedicated to the memory of Paulette Thomas Brown, one of my first schoolteachers who told me what I needed to know and not just what I wanted to hear; my mom, Mary Anne Sykes; and to my little girl, Macoia Azolé. Through her life, I realize why I must keep the light shining to guide and protect girls everywhere.

Acknowledgments

There has been nothing quite like writing this book. For many days and nights, it's been me, my pen, and the Holy Spirit. Friends, old and new, have held my hand on this awesome journey. I would like to thank Witchell Ward and Mary Anne Sykes for housing me from birth through young adulthood in an environment that allowed me to grow up, to be strong, and to learn from those around me. The students who avidly read *Mad Rhythms* magazine let me know how important I was to them, and consequently told me, "You need to do this book for us." Thank you for igniting my writing life.

I would like to thank my husband, Michael, for being by my side as I experienced every emotion in putting this book together. Every title, every piece of cover artwork, he reviewed. And he never complained. Michael, it's about time. And it's only the beginning. Thanks for believing and letting me be me.

I would like to thank Dr. Lois Benjamin for being the professor most responsible for turning me from a circular thinker into a critical, analytical one. Dr. Benjamin has believed in me since I was an uncertain undergraduate student at Hampton University. Her support continues to fuel the engine of my big dreams. I want to thank Tracy Grant, whose friendship is one of my greatest artistic and personal resources. He's my sounding board, he's the voice that tells me, "You can make it as an author, you got skill"; Chandra Sparks Taylor, my new friend and editor, whose incredible editing has given me more confidence than I could have ever imagined; Dave Goodson, who accepted me professionally and creatively from day one. My girls—Tamera Partin-Jones, Buffy Diggs-Williams, Sherelle Streetie-Preston, Shaconna Haley—are a fearless group of women who soldiered with me through the times in this book. My stories are their stories. Steve Wilson, my right hand, who supports every idea and puts all of his resources together to make it happen. My agent Marie Brown, whose reputation precedes her, read my work in its rawest and most unedited form. Although I was not her client at the time, she still took the time to encourage me with her response. Thanks, Marie. I really needed it. To Eric Blanding and Vince Bungi, my website and graphic artists thanks for bringing art to my words and visions.

I would like to thank Cherise Grant and the Simon & Schuster family for encouraging and believing in my blueprint for girls. To all the angels in the book business who assisted in the first launch of Blueprint: Karibu Books, Culture Plus, B. Dalton, Delta Sigma Theta, Johnnie Walker, Barnes & Noble, Radio One in Washington, Quality Books, National Book Network, and Special Occasions bookstore. Thanks also to Lee Bailey at RadioScope/EURweb.com, Michele Wright and Justine Love at WPGC, Nigel Alston and his *Motivational Moments* radio show, Yolanda Allen from Eden Bookstore and her radio program, Chris Askew of the *Unwrapped* radio program in Atlanta, *Black Beat* magazine, Jamie Foster Brown and Niki Turner of *Sister 2 Sister*, Joyce Davis of *Upscale* magazine, and India.Arie.

Much gratitude to my aunts Christine and Lana Gail, my cousin Madeline, and to women like Stella Ponzo, Brenda Bishop, Marlene Ridgeway, and Lois Rideout, who have gone before me and shown me the way through their actions, their words, and their strength.

Foreword

*J*n Yasmin Shiraz's inspirational guidebook, a new generation of women can rediscover timeless values to help navigate the sometimes perilous journey involved in coming of age. This invaluable blueprint dispenses pearls of wisdom about achievement, strong work ethic, dignity, self-respect, family solidarity, love, sexuality, personal responsibility, personal integrity, courage, and fortitude. This daughter of experience, a cohort of Generation X, has codified and made relevant for today's young women, in a manner that is far beyond her years, the wise counsels of foremothers who traditionally passed down their acumen and life's lessons through oral tradition.

At a time when younger women are being disconnected from their ancestral value system, one that helped in developing important coping skills and in equipping them with a clarity of course for charting life's rough seas, this guidebook is a welcome moral compass. Clearly, it can reconnect a younger generation to its roots, while serving as a bridge of hope to help them build a strong personal foundation to address future challenges.

A Senegalese proverb states, "The truth is like gold: keep it locked up and you will find it exactly as you first put it away." Shiraz has not locked up her golden nuggets for herself; instead, she has graciously given the passkey to others to unlock and share a treasure trove of time-tested truths.

Lois Benjamin, Ph.D.
Endowed University Professor of Sociology,
Hampton University
Author of *Black Elite: Facing the Color Line in the Twilight of the Twentieth Century* and *Three Black Generations at the Crossroads: Community, Culture and Consciousness*
Hampton, Virginia
December 2001

Introduction

*W*hen I was growing up as a teenager in America I had insecurities. I had dreams that I didn't know how to chase. And I had experiences with family, friends, school, and boys that I didn't understand. I wanted to tell somebody what I was going through but I didn't think they would understand. So I began writing about these things in my diaries. Somehow writing them down helped me to deal with them, solve them, and even get past some of the confusion and hurt. In college I faced tougher, more complex problems. Again I turned to my diaries. Jotting down my experiences in my journals has allowed me to look at what I was going through and to be real with myself. And through that process I repaired my self-esteem; I learned to aim high. And I got stronger. I'm still learning, and my journal remains a constant listener, problem solver, and confidant.

After graduating from Hampton University, I founded a college-circulated hip-hop magazine called *Mad Rhythms*. I visited several campuses to talk to college students about entertainment careers. At the end of my lectures young women came up to me to share their problems. Many of them were suffering with the same insecurities I had experienced, struggling with being misunderstood, dealing with family crises, and having problematic relationships with their boyfriends. They always asked for my advice. After these one-on-one discussions I went back to my hotel room and thought about the kinds of challenges that each young lady was facing. When I returned home I began searching through my old diaries for some of the answers. I figured I had survived many of the same issues; maybe my diary could help them find some answers. That's when a light went off in my head. I needed to write a book for my girls—girls who are facing dilemmas, need advice, and need to talk to somebody, just as I did.

Have you gone through something and wished someone had told you ahead of time how the problem could be avoided? Have people given you advice that you didn't realize was wrong until you felt it was too late to do anything about it? Have you felt isolated and alone in dealing with problems, like no one could understand where you're coming from? If you answer "yes" to any of these questions, then *The Blueprint for My Girls* will offer you comfort, motivation, and solutions.

I've separated the book into three phases: Foundation, Composition, and Fortification. Each phase contains various expressions that can assist you with analyzing, handling, and resolving challenges that come your way so that you can develop into a strong young woman. I've included my personal testimony on every page. Some of these diary entries were painful for me to share. With others, I was an outsider looking at how the people around me were behaving. All of these testimonies guided me in becoming the person I am today.

You may not relate to every entry, but there will be many that you can relate to. When you are going through an experience and need a source of strength, flip through the book again and see how I handled similar challenges. I've also included a testimony section with exercises that will help you get real with yourself regarding what is happening in your life. Learn from my mistakes. This book was written for you about your experiences, your trials, and your triumphs. This book is my journal from me to you. Use it as a solution getter, a problem solver, and a friend in need. My best hope is that reading about my experiences will help empower you to make the best possible decisions of your life.

Yasmin Shiraz
February 2004

PHASE I

Foundation

FOUNDATION—Your foundation is where you build who you are going to become in life. This will help you become a strong woman who can navigate life on her own terms.

expression 1

Say what's on your mind.

There are thoughts that we have that are never shared because we're afraid of how we are going to be perceived or if others will agree. There are people on this earth who will live seventy years, and no one will know what they stood for or what they represented because they never said what was on their minds.

MY TESTIMONY

I don't like sensing danger. It took me about fifteen years to articulate that to anyone. I don't like being in areas where I anticipate accidents. I don't favor going to playgrounds and seeing children playing when they are not supervised. I don't enjoy going to pools when the lifeguards are not thinking about saving anyone's life. My family always used to chalk this up to quirkiness, but it wasn't quirkiness. It was a deep feeling that I had. Now that I have told my family how I feel, they understand my position a lot better.

BLUEPRINT

God gave me my voice. I must use it to speak.

YOUR TESTIMONY

Think of a time when you didn't say what was on your mind but you should have. Jot down what you should have said. Now go in front of the mirror and loudly say what you've written down. Hear your voice.

expression 2

Be a person of hope.

*W*hen everything around you looks bleak, be a person of hope. Even if your heart is broken again and again, be a person of hope. And when you're tired of trying and your strength is gone, be a person of hope.

MY TESTIMONY

At twenty-four years of age, I decided to start an entertainment magazine. I didn't know enough about publishing to be discouraged; instead, I hoped that the business would lead to a full life for me. I had never taken any classes on magazine publishing, and I didn't have any connections in the entertainment business. I believed that I could work hard enough for people to give me a chance. I trusted that entering the entertainment business on my own would lead me to network with kindred souls who could assist me in realizing my goals. I didn't know if it would happen for sure, but I continued ambitiously. Now, years later, after trying times in the magazine publishing industry, I realize that my aspirations have been the strength and the light that have led me to a greater path. And, in the days when things weren't going my way, I really wouldn't have had anything if I didn't have hope.

BLUEPRINT

I will live my life as a person full of hope.

YOUR TESTIMONY

What would you like to happen to you, your life, and/or your environment? Write down at least three things and write down three reasons why these things should happen to you.

expression 3

Be thankful for everything.

$\mathscr{B}$e thankful for all that you have. There are always people who will have more than you. But then, there are always those who will have less. There is no sense in complaining about what we don't have.

MY TESTIMONY

When I was a little girl, my dad would come home and give me fifty-cent pieces. These were the coins with President John F. Kennedy featured on the head. It didn't have to be a special occasion or anything. In return, I wrote him poems about how great a father he was and how thankful I was for the coins. As I made friends in middle school, I realized many of them didn't know who their fathers were and some friends had horrible, abusive relationships with their fathers. I can remember taking my dad for granted, even though I had written those poems, but the more that I understood how special having a relationship with your father is, the more thankful I was for mine.

BLUEPRINT

I will spend more time being thankful for everything that I have.

YOUR TESTIMONY

What are the things that you are most thankful for? What would your life be like if you didn't have them?

expression 4

Do what you say.

*P*eople like to know that you can be counted on. There are so many unreliable individuals in the world that folks are actually thirsting for those who can be held to their word.

MY TESTIMONY

Even though I love my father, he has a way of saying that he's going to do something, and then when I'm really looking forward to it, he pulls out of the commitment. Some of his reasons for reneging on his promises are good. Some are bad. Over the years, I've come to rely less and less on what he says. He might state that he's coming to visit for my birthday every day for six months, but I don't believe him until I see him on the doorstep. I will always love my father, but our relationship has no strength in verbal commitment.

BLUEPRINT

When I say that I am going to do something, I will do it.

YOUR TESTIMONY

What was the last promise that you broke? Why did you go back on your word? How did it make you feel?

expression 5

Tell somebody when somebody does you wrong.

*W*e complain to ourselves, we complain to our parents, but when something really happens to us, when we should write to our senator or to the owner of the store or to the police department, we do not complain enough.

MY TESTIMONY

I dropped a friend off at his house one day after work. We were temporary employees for the U.S. Post Office. We had been sitting in the car in front of his house talking for about twenty minutes when a patrol car pulled up behind us and an officer demanded that I get out. I did what I was told and asked the officer what I had done wrong. The police officer threw me in the back of his car and grilled me with twenty questions while my friend went in the house and told his mother. I knew that I hadn't done anything wrong, so I demanded his badge number to report him for harassing me. He told me that with my smart mouth, he'd take me down to the police station. I just sat there. After about fifteen minutes, the officer let me out of the car and that was it. I was never told why I was put in the car. The officer was wrong for detaining me, he was wrong for not giving me his badge number, he was wrong for throwing me in the back of his car. I was wrong because I didn't report this abusive behavior to the governor, to a senator, to the police chief, or to anybody. Instead, I cried and drove home.

BLUEPRINT

I will no longer keep silent when somebody does me wrong. It's the only way to prevent it from happening to somebody else.

YOUR TESTIMONY

Write an anonymous letter detailing a hurt that comes from your past. Find the authority that you should send it to. Send the letter.

expression 6

Think what you will.

$\mathcal{B}$e guided by your own mind, your own spirit, your own soul. Think freely. Consider why there's so much talk about the lyrics in rap music. Mull the effort to save the whales. Whatever crosses your mind, whatever tantalizes your spirit, is yours to contemplate.

MY TESTIMONY

I wrote my undergraduate thesis on battered women. I volunteered at a battered women's shelter to learn about what happens to women who are beaten by their husbands and loved ones. Do they fight back? What happens to their children? No one in my family ever talked about women being abused. But in watching television and studying sociology, I heard a few things about it. So, I decided to learn more about battered women. I was intrigued and inspired by what I uncovered. An appreciation for these women's experiences grew from my willingness to think about them.

BLUEPRINT

My thoughts, whether spoken or simply dreamed, are mine to cherish. Whatever I do, I will think.

YOUR TESTIMONY

Think about something funny, strange, wonderful, or exciting. Write it down.

I really think . . .

expression 7

Resist negative peer pressure.

*a*void people who thrive on getting people to do negative things. They don't care about the consequences of their actions or you. Do things that you would do without a crowd cheering you on.

MY TESTIMONY

By the time I became a senior in high school, I had been confronted and bullied so much that anyone who looked at me wrong was potentially gonna get a beat down. I had had enough. I surrounded myself with a group of friends who were as willing as I was to sock the next person's lights out. It was our comfort zone. When I graduated from high school, my "right to fight" mentality was left there. I didn't want to brawl anymore. Some of my friends wanted to continue to rumble like before, but I had to say no. Times had changed. It took a while to catch on, but I ushered in a new way of thinking among my group of friends.

BLUEPRINT

When faced with people trying to get me to do the wrong thing, I will begin a tidal wave showing them what the right thing is.

YOUR TESTIMONY

When was the last time you felt negative peer pressure? What happened? Why didn't you like it?

expression 8

Express yourself without asking permission.

Nothing is more exciting than to realize that you can form your own opinions and express them without having to ask permission. Maybe you really believe that there is no such thing as an inappropriate outfit. Maybe you believe that women should stay at home to raise their children. Maybe you believe that President Clinton was innocent or that President George W. Bush didn't steal the election. Whatever you believe is your right.

MY TESTIMONY

I told my entire sociology class that I felt having sex before there is a mutual commitment ruins a relationship's potential. My classmates, with their hormones raging, couldn't believe that I had said such a thing. My hormones were frenzied, too, but I had to say what I believed. I had seen too many friends with their hearts broken, and I had had my heart broken. It wasn't that I didn't want my classmates to have fun and express their individual freedom and governance over their bodies, but most of the people who I knew were having sex with guys to *make* the relationship serious. I had learned that if they had sex before the pairing was official, the likelihood of a lasting union was nonexistent. The guys got what they wanted and they moved on. Although my opinion wasn't the most popular thing to say, it was what I believed. It was my opinion, and I didn't ask anyone's permission.

BLUEPRINT

I have the power of my opinions. I will speak my thoughts freely.

YOUR TESTIMONY

What's the most unpopular opinion of yours, the one that hardly any of your friends agree with? Why do they disagree with you?

expression 9

You are pretty enough.

*M*en are forever telling women what they should look like. Men are telling you how to get your hair done and what kinds of clothes to wear and even the color that your nail polish should be. For everything that they are saying, what they aren't saying is: "If you don't do what I tell you, you don't measure up to my idea of beauty."

MY TESTIMONY

I dated a guy in college who was very caught up in the material world. He was from Philadelphia and was very fascinated by the West Coast. Upon his return from one of his trips there, he told me that I looked good for a girl on the East Coast, but West Coast girls were different. Basically, he told me that I didn't measure up to women on that side of the country. Okay! That wasn't exactly a confidence booster, but I kept moving on. A lot of guys will say things to you to make you feel insignificant, especially when they feel insecure. I know for a fact that I was the best-looking girlfriend that he had ever had, yet he wanted to make me think that if I moved to L.A., I couldn't get a date.

BLUEPRINT

I define beauty for myself. Beauty is what I believe it to be.

YOUR TESTIMONY

Write down your three favorite physical features. Why are these your favorites?

Be a person with good morals and solid values.

*I*t is important to understand why integrity is necessary to be a strong person. In order to guide the way people are treated, society must have a universal code of ethics. Principles keep people in line.

MY TESTIMONY

During my junior year in college, my next-door neighbor used to hit his girlfriend. Kesha was petite, barely weighing one hundred pounds. Her boyfriend was about five-nine and at least eighty-five pounds heavier. When he got mad, he would slap her in the face in front of his housemates. Disgusted with his behavior, his friends would leave him and visit me and my housemates next door. They visited us, but they would never tell their friend that it was wrong to beat his girlfriend. When I asked why they didn't say anything, they always hid under the excuse of "not getting involved." Initially, I didn't understand why they didn't want to get involved.

After long conversations among us about domestic violence, these guys weren't sure one hundred percent if Derrick hitting Kesha was wrong.

BLUEPRINT

I possess solid values and good morals. Right will always be on my side.

YOUR TESTIMONY

When have you stood up for what's right? Why did you feel that it was necessary? What do you think are your best values?

expression *11*

Accept who you are.

*O*ur experiences shape who we are, and ultimately shape who we will become. There are people who come from different places, who know different things than you do, but you know what you know and they know what they know. We didn't all enter this life at the same location, so even our entrance has shaped the kind of people we become.

MY TESTIMONY

I grew up in a predominantly white suburb in Delaware. My mother grew up poor in an African-American community in North Carolina. Although my father grew up among the working black middle class of North Carolina, both of my parents instilled their experiences in me and my brother while they raised us. They didn't want us to know poverty. They didn't want us to know racial discrimination. They did everything that they could to insulate us and to ensure that we were educated. I am a product of my environment and of my upbringing. I can't talk to you about growing up as a Kennedy or as a Valley girl, but I can tell you about growing up as a Delaware girl. There are times when I've wanted to be like a Kennedy or like a girl who grew up in the Valley, but then there are times when I benefited most from growing up exactly as I did.

BLUEPRINT

I will accept my experiences and my history. God knows where I started and is with me all the way.

YOUR TESTIMONY

What are your favorite things? What's your family like? What are your favorite hobbies? What are you surrounded by?

expression 12

Your faith is between you and God.

*W*hen we hear a sermon, we often become so involved in the messenger that the message becomes second place. Then, if a scandal erupts and we find out that the pastor is less than an angel, we seem to lose our faith.

MY TESTIMONY

I knew a preacher once who used to abuse his wife. I don't believe that men should beat their wives. The preacher spoke very quietly and seemed very timid. He was an associate of mine who believed that he had to smack his wife around in order to get her full cooperation. I met another reverend whom I believe molested his children. His sons walked around like they carried hundred-ton secrets. In the course of my life, I've met many preachers, ministers, and reverends whose actions I have questioned. I remember going to a church in Maryland, attending regularly, then realizing that the church and the ministry were a sham. At that point, I gave up my faith in ministers entirely. Sometime later, I realized that my faith didn't have to be in spiritual leaders. My faith is in God. My relationship is with God.

BLUEPRINT

I realize that the messenger is just a vessel to get the message heard. I will pay more attention to the message rather than the messenger.

YOUR TESTIMONY

Write a letter to God revealing five things that have been happening in your life. Tell God what you think about organized religion.

expression 13

Listen when people talk to you.

Stop everything that you're doing and concentrate on what's happening around you. If people knew how much they could learn by observing, the whole world would probably stop talking. But instead, we are often so caught up with sounding intelligent and getting our own agendas across that we undervalue the art of listening.

MY TESTIMONY

My aunt Nora and I would often have talking competitions when she would spend the night. We would see who could talk the most before falling asleep. Although my aunt was more than thirty years older than I was, I never let her win. I was young and too absorbed in my side of the conversation. As I reflect on the experiences and stories that she must have been sharing with me in our talking contests, I realize that I wasn't even listening.

BLUEPRINT

Listening allows me to absorb what others are thinking and feeling and exposes me to another worldview.

YOUR TESTIMONY

What's a really good thing that someone told you or that you heard recently? Why are you glad that you heard it?

expression 14

Set high standards for yourself.

*W*hen you don't push yourself, you are met with mediocre results. If you endeavor to do things that you haven't done before, you'll get farther. Don't be afraid to challenge yourself.

MY TESTIMONY

I never personally knew anyone who owned a magazine before I started mine. For that reason alone many individuals told me that I shouldn't attempt to publish one. People didn't think that I would know what I was doing. It seemed that folks didn't think that I was smart enough to figure it out. I started an entertainment magazine business anyway. I learned things that I didn't know. And, of course, I made mistakes. But each day with the business I continued to push myself farther and farther and harder and harder.

BLUEPRINT

I won't be afraid to set high standards for myself.

YOUR TESTIMONY

Think about what you want to do with your life. What do you feel challenged by?

I feel challenged when I think about doing . . .

expression 15

Strive for excellence.

*M*ediocrity is a word found in the dictionary, but outside of its purpose there, being second-rate has no place in society. Live in bold colors. Strive for excellence.

MY TESTIMONY

I remember my first job as a summer intern at Hockessin Community Center in Delaware. It was an office assignment where I learned how to take complete messages, how to follow instructions, and how to be professional at all times. In this occupation, I worked with economically disadvantaged residents in the Hockessin community. I would prepare care packages, take food to the residents' homes, and accept clothing donations. As the summer was coming to a close, the director of the community center told me that my work ethic was better than that of many people who were much older. At thirteen years old, I wondered how that could be possible. When I asked the director, she told me, "Some people take pride in their work and some people don't. Just because someone is older doesn't necessarily mean that he will do a better job." Those words forever changed the way that I go about my tasks. Pursuits then became about excellence and not experience. So as I went from one job to the next, I never allowed my lack of seasoning to affect my confidence at work. For me, it was all about quality.

BLUEPRINT

Instead of accepting mediocrity, I must strive to be an example of excellence.

YOUR TESTIMONY

Was there ever a time in your life when you didn't do your best and you could have done better? When? If you had done better, how would your life have changed?

expression 16

Be able to say you're sorry.

What makes apologies so difficult? What makes saying sorry so laborious? Maybe it's hard because we fear that our penitence won't be accepted. Maybe it's rough because we believe more discussion will arise out of our atonement. Whether you're in the right or in the wrong, or whether you have to say sorry, apologies are the bridges over troubled waters.

MY TESTIMONY

"You're not really my brother," I recall saying to my only sibling when I was in the ninth grade. I was so caught up in making new friends and forging relationships with people whom I desperately wanted to like me that I didn't care about hurting my brother's feelings. One day he told my mother what I was saying. Clearly, he didn't appreciate me disowning him for people who I didn't really know. Too stubborn to apologize, I continued to argue with him about something else. Today, I realize that I should have said that I was sorry. And to his credit, I know my real brother's place in my life, yet I have no idea where all of those pretend brothers have gone.

BLUEPRINT

I will be encouraged to apologize when my heart tells me. More pain is erased from giving an apology than the pain that is caused from withholding one.

YOUR TESTIMONY

Who should you have apologized to but didn't? Write down what you should have said. Be willing to read your apology to the person.

expression 17

Don't give in to suicidal thoughts.

$\mathcal{P}$erhaps, during the moment when we think that our life will not get better, we consider suicide. Maybe we think that we'll never experience happiness again. We're depressed and have decided in our minds that life won't get better, but we don't know that. Life is full of ups and downs. When we give in to suicidal thoughts, we give up on life.

MY TESTIMONY

My mother's friend's son killed himself when he was twelve years old. He hadn't even begun to live, but he was already fed up with life. I don't recall if he was mad at his parents or if he was having difficulty at school, but I know his death devastated his mother. Her life was never the same again. Part of her hurt was because she knew something about living that her son didn't comprehend. If he had allowed himself to live even five years more, the trouble that he experienced at twelve would have seemed unimportant. If he had allowed himself to live ten more years, his problems at twelve probably would have seemed irrelevant.

BLUEPRINT

Nothing in my life is going to stay the same, but I am willing to let life take its course.

YOUR TESTIMONY

How does your life impact your mom, friends, or other family members?

My life is important because . . .

expression 18

Accept people as they are.

*I*f everybody in the world were exactly alike, then life would be extremely boring. In theory, opposites attract, but at the same time people feel uncomfortable with those who are different. Appreciating the diversity of others is like learning how to get up on a new side of the bed in the morning. It's not a big deal. It just adds some spice to your life.

MY TESTIMONY

I recall having a colleague who was unusually difficult to get along with. Despite how nice people were to him, he always had an attitude. Many colleagues had to work on various projects with Alex, and tensions always arose. After many discussions, Alex confided that he was a homosexual, biracial male who grew up being criticized and ridiculed. By the time he entered adulthood, he decided that he wasn't going to give anybody the chance to dislike him; he was going to dislike others first. Had somebody accepted Alex early on in his life, he'd probably be a whole lot more good-natured today.

BLUEPRINT

I will learn how to accept people as they are, with all of their differences.

YOUR TESTIMONY

Name someone whom you hardly know but you don't like. Why don't you like that person? Now forget that you don't know them.

expression 19

Choose your friends wisely.

*J*ust being around certain people makes others think that you're that kind of person. If you're around individuals who are viewed positively, you'll be thought of positively. And if you are around persons who are viewed negatively, you'll be thought of negatively. We are able to choose our companions, and we should do so wisely.

MY TESTIMONY

In middle school, junior high, and high school, it seemed like choosing friends was more a question of who was sitting next to you in a classroom. It didn't really seem like I made a conscious decision regarding who was my friend. But in college, things were different. I was very selective about the people with whom I hung out. I found someone who could help me look inwardly. I picked a person who could help me be more fashionable. Then, I opted for people who would assist me in studying harder. I realized that these friends would help make the difference in my college experience.

BLUEPRINT

With friends, I can choose people who complement me, who make me stronger, who help me to become a better person.

YOUR TESTIMONY

What are good qualities that you want in your friends? What are some of the things that you like about your current friends?

expression 20

Be careful whom you confide in.

*a*t different times in our lives, we feel the need to confide in others with the hope of receiving a good
sounding board. The need to have faith in people is a part
of who we are. And, because of its importance, we must
take extra care in selecting the people we confide in.

MY TESTIMONY

My mother had a childhood friend in whom she
believed she could confide. They had grown up in the
same neighborhood and attended the same schools, so
my mother thought that she had a best friend whom
she could really trust. As a teenager she confided in
Belinda and later found that Belinda did not keep her
secret. From that point on, my mother hasn't been big
on sharing secrets and definitely not on trusting people.

BLUEPRINT

I will be careful about the people I select to confide in.

YOUR TESTIMONY

Create a small notebook for your secrets. Instead of telling somebody your private thoughts, write them down in your notebook. Let a week pass. If the urgency to tell someone your secret has gone away, rip up the page of your notebook that contains the secret.

expression 21

Trust yourself.

When something just ain't right—maybe it's a feeling in your side, perhaps it's something in your head that makes you twist, but whatever it is, it just ain't right—all of these things are telling you to go with your gut or to stop and rethink what you were about to do.

MY TESTIMONY

Looking for a job in the wild, crazed city of Washington, D.C., can be daunting. Applying for a marketing job with a small start-up firm, I was interviewed by a lady who gave off a bizarre vibe and who didn't exactly give eye contact. In our follow-up interview she wore a biker outfit and put her feet up on the table. Something told me that this small firm wasn't going to be as professional as it should be. I felt the hint, but I ignored it. Two months later, the company cheated me out of five hundred dollars.

BLUEPRINT

I will learn to trust myself and react as if God were tapping me on the shoulder.

YOUR TESTIMONY

When was the last time you heard a voice in your head or an alarm going off?

I felt funny when . . .

expression 22

Avoid he say/she sayers.

*P*eople who spend most of their time talking about others are spending too much time doing nothing.

MY TESTIMONY

During my freshman year in high school, there was a girl, Lyndell, who approached me every week with, "I heard that you were talking about me." Mind you, I never talked about her to my friends or anyone. Days after she'd confronted me, she would try to be friendly. As the year wore on, she and her two other friends would want to talk to me in the cafeteria and ask, "Did you talk about me?" It went on for a full year until Lyndell finally became so confrontational that I beat her up in front of our school building. When I became a senior in high school, Lyndell and her friends wanted to be cool with me, but I didn't want to be bothered because I knew what they were all about—nothing.

BLUEPRINT

I will avoid people who spend too much time talking about others.

YOUR TESTIMONY

Who do you know who talks about others all the time? How do you feel when you hear all those things being said? Do you ever think you could be the topic of discussion?

When I hear gossip about others . . .

Know right from wrong.

*W*henever I am confused about doing the right thing, I ask, "How would I feel if someone were doing this to me?" Any time I'm not sure of what's right, I question myself, "What would it feel like if it were me?"

MY TESTIMONY

I remember going to a high school dance with one of my girlfriends. A guy who saw that my boyfriend wasn't around tried to hit on me. Even though I could have flirted with Tony, I politely told him, "You're cool and everything, but I'm not interested." Tony knew my boyfriend and he may have been genuinely interested in me, but I felt that I wouldn't have wanted my boyfriend to flirt with someone when I wasn't around. It wasn't the right thing to do.

BLUEPRINT

I know right from wrong. I will consider how I would feel if someone were doing to me what I'm thinking about doing to them.

YOUR TESTIMONY

What is one thing that you've seen people do that you know is wrong? What have you done in your past that you thought was right at the time but now feel is wrong?

When I did . . .

expression 24

Know your father.

*a*bsentee fathers seem to be the cultural norm these days. Who can explain the relationships that men are having with their babies' mamas? Despite popular belief, good fathers do exist. Often because of our fathers' bad relationships with our mothers, we develop bad relationships with our fathers.

MY TESTIMONY

After nineteen years of marriage my mother and father divorced. Though I did not live with my father afterward he is a very positive figure in my life. He is particular about his personal appearance, garnering a "Best Dressed" award when he was a senior in high school. He has a quick temper and sometimes he likes to argue. It's a part of his personality. I don't always agree with the decisions that my father makes, but because I know him, I understand why he makes them.

BLUEPRINT

The more that I know about my father, the more that I learn about myself. I will endeavor to familiarize myself with my father and his history.

YOUR TESTIMONY

What do you know about your father? Can you talk to him? If not, who can help you contact your father? If you don't want to talk to him, why not? Write a letter to your father asking him about his life as a teenager. Send it.

expression 25

Finish what you start.

a masterpiece that the painter doesn't complete is a half done painting. A quilt that is half done will not keep you warm on a cold winter's night. Have the courage to not only start something but to finish it as well.

MY TESTIMONY

I used to start book projects and before it came time to finish, I would focus on something else. Months after I prematurely left an undertaking, it would begin haunting me. The thought of not completing the work planted doubts in my mind. Could I have ever finished the book? Would it have been good? Before long, I realized that although I physically left an idea, it didn't mean that I left the goal mentally. So I set forth to complete every task that I started, thereby eliminating any possibility of doubt that could grow from the work that I hadn't completed.

BLUEPRINT

Completing what I start gives me a sense of accomplishment, and it motivates me to begin and achieve other goals.

YOUR TESTIMONY

What project have you started but decided against finishing? Why didn't you finish it? Name a project that you want to finish. Tell yourself why this project is so important.

expression 26

Show your love.

*J*t should be easy to be the thoughtful person who gives gifts, bestows compliments, and showers affection on others. Those closest to us need to know how much we love them. When we are affectionate, thoughtful, and giving to our loved ones, they know how much they are appreciated.

MY TESTIMONY

My grandmother was put into a nursing home shortly before I entered graduate school. Although she lived four and a half hours from my house, I made a commitment to visit her every other weekend. At our first meetings, she knew who I was, and we talked about me going to graduate school and my new fiancé. But, as I got closer to entering graduate school, she began to fade. While she was living in the home, I could not afford to buy her fancy gifts or flowers or chocolates for every visit, but I gave her my time. She died six months after I finished graduate school. A lot of my other family members would say that they were going to visit my grand-mother or that they were going to send her something to brighten up her room, but all she really wanted was for people to visit her and show her how much they loved her by being there with her.

BLUEPRINT

I can give of myself and of my heart. It's the sincerest act of my love.

YOUR TESTIMONY

Which three people in your life need to know that you love them? Write their names down. What can you do to show them?

expression 27

Be passionate about everything you do.

$\mathcal{B}$ eing passionate is one of the greatest assets that you can have in life. The student who is having trouble understanding the course assignment but is working hard and meeting with the instructor will be met with success. Dedication will get you over the hump.

MY TESTIMONY

As a sociology student in college, I didn't always get straight As. Sometimes the subject matter was so complex that I didn't grasp it, but I asked questions in class and I met with the instructors. Regardless of what I didn't understand, I didn't want my instructors to think that I wasn't trying. I was determined to learn. There were times when my grades were borderline, and because of my perseverance, I earned the higher grade. My instructors knew that whatever I lacked in clinical knowledge, I made up for by being dedicated.

BLUEPRINT

If I am passionate about what I do in life, success will follow.

YOUR TESTIMONY

Think about the things that you enjoy doing. What three things do you enjoy the most? Why do you enjoy them? Can you make a career out of doing these things?

expression 28

Ask for help.

a parable states, "To have to ask questions makes us look as if we haven't done our homework." But what happens when we really need assistance and there are people out there who can help us? We should ask for help when we need it, and we shouldn't feel like we're any less for it.

MY TESTIMONY

I wanted to select the right college for my master's program. I was living at home with my mom, and I did not want to take out student loans. I knew that I wanted to go on scholarship, but I had never applied for a scholarship. I called my former collegiate adviser and asked for her help. Not only was she able to assist me in narrowing down schools, she had a list of institutions that would cover the costs of my entire education. Thanks to her assistance, I did not contribute one dime for my graduate educational costs.

BLUEPRINT

There are people out there who want to help me, so I will ask for it.

YOUR TESTIMONY

Everybody has problems or things that they need help with. What things do you need help with? Name the people who you believe can help you with these challenges. Map out a time when you can ask for their help.

I need help on . . .

expression 29

Money doesn't guarantee happiness.

𝓘n American society, money is still being lauded as the entrée to happiness. People are still being taught that if we have "things" then our lives are going to be better. But most of us realize that rich people are not necessarily the happiest.

MY TESTIMONY

One of the first jobs I accepted after college was low paying. I excelled in the position, but I wasn't exuberant because I wasn't challenged. I accepted the gig because I needed a source of income. Soon after, I started looking for employment that would give me the experience that I wanted. I didn't focus on pay, yet I ended up making more money in the next job. But even when I had secured a nice salary, I wasn't completely gratified because I wasn't doing the kind of job I had dreamed of for myself. I had money and a nice sports car, but I wasn't happy. I realized that unless I was doing what I was most enthusiastic about, then no amount of money would make me content.

BLUEPRINT

When I set goals for myself, I won't be limited by the amount of money that I can make. Instead, I will surround myself with opportunities that can bring about happiness on personal, mental, social, and physical levels.

YOUR TESTIMONY

Read an entertainment or music magazine that you like. Read a couple of articles about rich people who you like. What kinds of negative things were reported about their lives?

I read that _____ [celebrity] . . .

expression 30

Don't waste time judging others.

Spending time criticizing people is a waste of energy. Folks always want to sit on the corner talking about what others' lives are like. The energy we spend critiquing should be used to improve our own current situation.

MY TESTIMONY

Angelique was a quiet girl whom I had known since sixth grade. In middle school, we sat at the same table for lunch. We talked during recess. We were good friends. On the weekends, we visited each other. When we went to high school Angelique's disposition switched. She was quieter and far more reserved. She didn't seem as outgoing and she became a loner. I liked her as much as I always had, but I couldn't figure out why she seemed different. One day in our eleventh-grade sex-education class, we saw a film on rape and child molestation. During the film, Angelique screamed and left the room. Though puzzled at the time by this outburst, I later found out that Angelique's mother's boyfriend had been raping her after school. I didn't start to dislike Angelique or judge her because her disposition had changed. She needed a friend more than she needed someone to judge her.

BLUEPRINT

I don't really know about what others are going through enough to judge them. I will spend my precious time doing other things.

YOUR TESTIMONY

What are some things that people have thought about you that are wrong? What are some things that you have thought about people and later found out were incorrect?

People used to think that I was . . .

Ask questions.

*I*f you don't understand something, ask. Don't sit in the back of the class afraid to speak up. We cannot learn if we do not inquire. Asking questions does not mean that you are less intelligent, it simply means that you are endeavoring to know more.

MY TESTIMONY

One of my first electives as a freshman in college was African history. The teacher would ramble about this tribe, that tribe, this part of history, this slave trade, and so forth. Listening to him made me fall asleep. I sat in the back of the class and, on most days, I didn't know what the specific topic was. I would sit for fifty minutes, three times a week, and I wouldn't have a real idea of what the professor was talking about. I didn't ask one single question. I didn't help anyone else by remaining silent. Since I ultimately failed the class, I know that I didn't help myself. If I had the opportunity to take that class again, I'd sit up front and I'd be inquisitive. No matter how boring, I would learn that subject matter.

BLUEPRINT

I am not fooling anyone by pretending to know things I don't know. I will ask questions.

YOUR TESTIMONY

Think about a time in class when you didn't understand something. What was it that you didn't understand? Why didn't you ask a question? If you had asked some questions, how would your experience about that class have been different?

I shoulda asked . . .

expression 32

Don't burn bridges.

Sometimes when people anger you, you want nothing more than to cut off the relationship. Forget about parting on good terms, they did something that you didn't like and now you don't want to have anything to do with them.

MY TESTIMONY

You never know when people can help you. During my college summers, I worked at the U.S. Postal Service headquarters in Washington, D.C. One year, I worked for the historian, another year I worked for the inspector general. Each summer I would work hard, but I would have a supervisor of whom I wasn't particularly fond. No matter how I was treated, or if I believed something unfair had occurred, I remained in good standing at my summer job. When spring would begin and it was time for me to look for a new position at the post office, I could call my previous supervisor and either be rehired or referred to another department. In the end, how I felt personally about my supervisors didn't matter. I wanted to be sure that I could get a paycheck.

BLUEPRINT

Everyone who I've ever come across may be in a position to help me one day, even the people I don't like. I will put personal feelings aside, keep the lines of communication open, and keep the bridge sturdy.

YOUR TESTIMONY

When is the last time you burned a bridge? Has burning a bridge affected a friendship?

_____ *and I used to be friends but . . .*

expression 33

People have "isms."

For every leaf on every tree that has ever lived, there is a reason for someone not to like you. It's almost as if people spend time creating "isms." Don't-like-anyone-ism, you're-not-tall-enough-ism, don't-like-the-color-of-your-hair-ism, women-are-inferior-ism, you're-not-middle-class-ism. Some people won't like you because of how you look or how you dress or because of your physical abilities, your aptitude, or your attitude.

MY TESTIMONY

I've tried to make friends with people who did not want to be my buddies. In a ninth-grade social studies class, a girl told me, "You look like you always have something smart to say." My look was reason enough for her not to become friends with me. Truthfully, I didn't always have something smart to say. Throughout middle school and high school, I would meet people who already had their minds made up about me. Because of what I looked like or how I dressed, they already knew whether they could like me. It was their isms about me.

BLUEPRINT

I will try hard not to be one of those people who keeps isms going about other people. As I go through life and people have their isms concerning me, I won't worry about it, I'll keep moving on.

YOUR TESTIMONY

Write down some isms that you think exist.

People who . . .

expression 34

Be able to explain your actions.

*H*ave you ever done things that people who were looking from the outside couldn't believe? Have you ever been scolded for your actions, and then after you explained, people saw the other side of the story? When people are on the outside of a situation attempting to analyze it, they often don't get the full picture. They make judgments against us without having all of the facts.

MY TESTIMONY

Accusing an instructor of abusing his power and discriminating against a student is no small feat. When I was thrust into that situation as a graduate student, I had to ask myself, "Should I fight this professor? And, if I retaliate against him, what do I win?" I began to talk to my most treasured counsel about what I should do. Most people instructed me to not challenge the professor. One person advised me otherwise. Despite the guidance that I received, after I shared my reasons for confronting the teacher, my advisers understood why I had to resist, even if they didn't agree with me.

BLUEPRINT

Even if my decisions seem unpopular, I should still be able to explain my actions. My explanation can bring others closer to my situation.

YOUR TESTIMONY

When was the last time a parent or friend was mad at you because of something you did? Sincerely explain yourself and what happened. Write it down. The parent or friend shouldn't be mad at you after reading this explanation.

expression 35

Sex complicates things.

Social scientists call it "casual sex." But nothing about sex is casual. Copulation to one person means commitment and to another person it means fun. Lovemaking to one person means "call me tomorrow." Coitus to another person means "I won't call you ever again." You never know exactly what sex means to the other person until after you've had it.

MY TESTIMONY

Everything was going just fine in my relationship with Edward. We went to the movies. We went out to dinner. We talked on the phone for hours, just discussing each of our families. We would sit on the floor in front of the television watching movies. We both liked each other a lot, and we were focused on being friends and getting to know each other. One night after watching movies and hanging out, Edward and I decided to become intimate. The next night, Edward changed. He wanted to know where I was every minute of the day. He wanted to be informed of what I was doing and whom I was with. I didn't know it before, but sex to Edward meant ownership. We were already boyfriend and girlfriend, but now Edward wanted to own me.

BLUEPRINT

I can ruin all the fun that I am having by beginning a sexual relationship. Intercourse can come later.

YOUR TESTIMONY

What does having sex mean to you? Would your relationship be more serious if you have sex?

I think having sex should . . .

PHASE 2

Composition

COMPOSITION—Your composition is where you arrange your life options, decisions, challenges, and experiences to assist in preparing yourself for womanhood. It's designed to make you a powerful, self-determined, and self-loving individual.

expression 36

Don't become obsessed with weight.

*W*eight continues to be an obsession in American culture. In our minds, it seems that we can never be skinny enough and that we are always obese or potentially overweight.

MY TESTIMONY

While growing up, whenever I went to the doctor and was weighed, I was told that my weight was "normal for a child my age." As a young person, I looked into the mirror and saw a person who I liked. I didn't see someone who needed plastic surgery. When I entered college, I worked out using weights and cardiovascular machines because I had learned so much about exercise in health class. I also learned that women should have a healthy attitude about who we are. A healthy attitude is not just what you look like, it's also what you feel.

BLUEPRINT

I will not become obsessive about my weight for cosmetic reasons.

YOUR TESTIMONY

How do you feel about your weight? Can you do anything to have a better outlook about your weight?

I think my size . . .

expression 37

Career aspirations change.

From childhood to adulthood, you may decide to reassess what you aspire to be. When you were four, you thought that you'd grow up to be a doctor. When you were twelve, you decided that you wanted to become a dancer. When you turned eighteen, you realized that you didn't know what you wanted to be. That's okay.

MY TESTIMONY

When I entered college, I believed that I wanted to be a journalist. Somewhere between my freshman year and my junior year, I decided that I wanted to be an entertainment lawyer. By the time that I was preparing myself for graduation, I thought I wanted to be a screenwriter. At least once a year, I changed my mind about my profession. Each time, I learned more about what I really wanted to do. My aspirations changing didn't show me that I didn't know who I was, they gave me proof that I did.

BLUEPRINT

As my career aspirations change, I realize that I'm learning more about myself.

YOUR TESTIMONY

What is the first job you want to have? What kind of job do you want when you get older? Which jobs do you like?

I like _____ because . . .

expression 38

Being alone is not a death sentence.

Women who are desperate when they don't have a companion think that being alone is a terminal disease. Some people believe that the only way to have happiness is to be with another person. However, when you are alone, you are able to concentrate on your desires, your shortcomings, and the priorities in your life.

MY TESTIMONY

I started dating when I was fifteen. Once I began, it seemed like I was on a roll. As one union ended, I was already beginning another one. This cycle went on for years. Before I could get over the pain from one bond, I was on to another. Then, a relationship ended that truly broke my heart, and only by being by myself could I put the pieces back together. I elected to be alone and I found strength in learning what I liked, what I did not like, and what I wanted to do in my spare time. I was alone, but I learned about me.

BLUEPRINT

I will cherish the times when I have the opportunity to be alone.

YOUR TESTIMONY

Do I need to be in a relationship? Why or why not? What do I enjoy doing by myself?

I think relationships . . .

expression **39**

Everybody who you like doesn't necessarily like you.

*W*hy is it that opposites attract? Why is it that people want to be liked by the very folks who don't want to like them? In our journey through life, we come across all kinds of folks. We meet those whom we bestow our affection and respect upon even though they don't deserve it and even though our affection and respect will never be returned.

MY TESTIMONY

I remember a time my brother and I had a party at our house late one night. I was in ninth grade and he was in eleventh grade. We invited some acquaintances and some of our good friends over to just hang out with us. When it was time to draw the gathering to a close, our "acquaintances" became rowdy and didn't respect our house or our neighborhood. They left wine bottles and trash on the side of our lawn. They didn't care if they woke up the neighbors because they didn't value us and they didn't respect where we lived. We had invited them over to our house because we liked them and we had hoped that they would like us, but they didn't, and their actions showed it. We never invited those acquaintances to our house again, and we never eagerly bestowed our affection on individuals who didn't seem to be caring toward us.

BLUEPRINT

It's okay for people not to favor me, and it's okay for me not to associate with people who I know don't prefer me.

YOUR TESTIMONY

Have you been nice to someone who refused to be nice to you? Why do you think they are acting that way?

Even though I like . . .

expression 40

Family members aren't always our best advisers.

$\mathcal{F}$amily members can be a great source of information for a lot of life's ills. But advice is not "one size fits all," so your relatives are not always qualified to be the ultimate influence in all of your life decisions.

MY TESTIMONY

When I decided to go to graduate school, I asked family members to advise me. Some refused because they had no experience. Others told me what they had heard. Most of the advice that I received from family was not really on target with the higher education experience. The reason was simple: Many of my relatives hadn't experienced it, so they really couldn't advise me.

BLUEPRINT

Family members don't intentionally misguide me, but it happens. When facing career challenges, I will obtain advice from those who have the relevant experience.

YOUR TESTIMONY

Name three family members whom you ask for advice. Have they given you advice that you didn't agree with?

I received advice on . . .

expression 41

Always craving attention isn't healthy.

*P*eople noticing us makes us feel special. It's an important nod to our self-esteem. It's okay to want others to focus on us every now and then, but constantly craving attention will eventually lead to us attracting the wrong people.

MY TESTIMONY

I used to want a lot of time from everyone. Whenever I had a problem, I would consult with no fewer than three friends on the severity of the conundrum. Whenever I had issues at school or within a relationship, there I was, calling three people to help me. After a while, it seemed that my need to call several people undermined my confidence to solve dilemmas on my own. One day I decided that I wasn't going to call anybody to discuss my obstacles. Instead, I was going to sit down and come up with a solution on my own.

BLUEPRINT

I will love myself, spend time by myself, and crave less attention from others.

YOUR TESTIMONY

Are there times when you want more attention than others? It could be in a public place, in front of certain people, or when you're feeling a certain way.

I wanted extra attention when . . .

Life can be frustrating.

*a*s you go through life, no one can promise you that everything will go your way. No one can tell you that you won't get kicked in the teeth in your travels. Sometimes, when it seems that you are doing everything in your power to make progress, you'll probably have some doors slammed in your face. After so many doors close, even the most optimistic person can become frustrated.

MY TESTIMONY

High school for me wasn't exactly a picnic. As a result of bickering with my parents, peer pressure, and zits, I was ready to roll by the time graduation came. I had begun to apply to colleges and although I wasn't a straight-A student, I believed that my grades were acceptable. That was until the prestigious university that I applied to wrote, "You must go to precollege before we allow you into 'real' college." I immediately felt frustrated. Didn't the admissions department realize that getting out of high school was a chore in itself?

BLUEPRINT

Although frustration is going to come my way, I will stay strong. I know that with every closed door, I am steps closer to a rewarding opportunity.

YOUR TESTIMONY

When were you really frustrated? What makes you frustrated?

I was really frustrated when. . . .

I'm getting over my frustration by . . .

expression **43**

People will get ahead the wrong way.

*W*hen individuals progress by knowing someone and not because of their knowledge, it hurts those who have worked hard and who don't get ahead. Sometimes it's downright frustrating to see somebody doing nothing but getting accolades, but we can't be overly concerned with how others advance. We have to be concerned with how *we're* getting to the next level.

MY TESTIMONY

I accepted employment in the federal government for which I was told that I had to have a college degree. Several months later, I discovered that my supervisor did not complete college. She claimed her experience helped her to get her positions. As I continued to work in this office, I found that many of my supervisor's friends whom she had hired did not have a college degree either. I was really frustrated when I realized that I was in a lower-paying position, and I had more education than my supervisor and many of my coworkers.

BLUEPRINT

Life isn't always fair, but I can't focus on what others are doing. I have to strategize my own plan for success.

YOUR TESTIMONY

What situations have you witnessed personally that you felt were unfair? What do you think should have happened?

I thought it was unfair when . . .

expression 44

Coping with death isn't easy.

The pain subsides, but often never goes away. When we lose loved ones, we are stricken with grief, we are looking for the suffering to ease itself, but it seems like it never does.

MY TESTIMONY

My tenth-grade geometry teacher died about three years after I completed graduate school. Mrs. Bramble remained a mentor and a friend to me long after I left high school. When I talked to her regarding my writing career, she always encouraged me. I used to dream about the day when she would ride with me to a gala in my honor at which I would thank her for always supporting me. When she died, I knew that the dream of our limo ride would exist only in my mind. The way that she lived her life and the way that she always treated me continues to live in mine. I cherish my memories of Mrs. Bramble. I continue to experience sadness because I can't speak with her and because I can't visit with her, but everybody in life has to go sometime. It comforts me to know that Mrs. Bramble left because she had to and not because she wanted to.

BLUEPRINT

Feeling pain helps me know how much I have loved. I realize that it is part of my coping, part of my healing.

YOUR TESTIMONY

Who in your life has passed away? Why do you miss him or her? How can you honor their memory?

It would make _____ happy if I did . . .

expression **45**

Allow yourself to communicate.

Sometimes it is hard to discuss things. Talking can be so painful that sometimes we don't even want to consider it. Only through communication are we able to rid ourselves of problems. Disagreements and unresolved feelings can be worked out through discussion. When we refuse to converse, we refuse to allow ourselves to move beyond the pain.

MY TESTIMONY

One of my best friends and I hadn't talked for six years. I had been going through changes in my personal life and I needed that time to evaluate my friendships. I had undergone so much pain as a result of confusion that I built a wall around myself that shut her out. I felt such anguish and sadness regarding our relationship that I couldn't talk about it. The words wouldn't come. After each conflict—before we stopped talking—I refused to discuss my hurt, and with each miscommunication, another part of the wall was built. Before I knew it, the wall was so high and thick, I couldn't get over it or walk around it.

BLUEPRINT

I can communicate. The only way for me to resolve agonizing issues is to talk through them.

YOUR TESTIMONY

You have a situation that is difficult to discuss. Why is it difficult to talk about? What would make it less difficult?

I don't like discussing _____ because . . .

expression 46

Understand the gift of being female.

Today's woman generally does not know how special being a woman is. She does not understand her power, her sensibilities, or her relationship to the entire universe. It's sad to see women who don't understand the gift. But the women who do have the world in the palms of their hands.

MY TESTIMONY

Throughout my life, I have been told by many guys that "I'm different." I've been told, "Other girls don't think about that kind of stuff." On dates, I've demanded respect. The guys who I've met have been intrigued by my presence. In dealing with them, I never pretended that everything was okay if it wasn't. I didn't want to be the victim in anybody's fantasy. A guy liked me in college, and during one of our first meetings, he groped one of my butt cheeks as a joke. I punched him in the eye as hard as I could, while at the same time kicking him in the knee. He never thought groping was a joke again.

The guys who I've come across, I've always wanted to leave with a positive feeling about women. I've always felt that it was my responsibility.

BLUEPRINT

If I, as a woman, demand respect from everyone I deal with, it ensures that other women will be respected, too.

YOUR TESTIMONY

What are some of the best things about being a girl? Write down why you like being a girl.

I like being a girl because . . .

expression 47

People will desert you.

$\mathcal{P}$eople will turn their backs on you at your lowest point. Maybe it's human nature, perhaps it's the manifestation of fear. Whatever it is, low times will come, and during these dispirited periods you may actually be alone. You may want someone to lean on and find that no one will be there.

MY TESTIMONY

From ages sixteen to twenty, I experienced a tremendous amount of personal problems. My dilemmas were emotional, financial, social, and physical. They were calls for help. They were acts of desperation. During this four-year period, I never talked to my parents about what was really bothering me. It's not that I didn't try. I distinctly remember calling my mother to discuss my latest problem, but when she would hear a certain tone in my voice, she would hurry me off the phone. As the dial tone sounded in my ear, I would sit in my dorm room, with tears streaming down my face. Through my tears, I realized that I was alone in solving whatever predicament I had.

BLUEPRINT

Sometimes blue periods make other people run in the opposite direction. I realize that it's not anything against me personally.

YOUR TESTIMONY

When have you felt deserted by the people you were counting on? Why do you think they deserted you?

I felt by myself when . . .

expression **48**

Change always comes.

$\mathcal{W}$e can make change come at a certain time, or we can wait for it to overtake us. Why do we fight transitioning so much? Conceivably, we fight change because we don't want to deal with the unfamiliar; however, we should be more welcoming of movement because it is surely going to come whether we like it or not.

MY TESTIMONY

When my mother told my brother and me that she was moving from Delaware to Maryland, we thought it was the worst possible news that we could receive. After all, we had grown up in Delaware and all of our friends lived there. We were nineteen and seventeen years of age, respectively. How were we going to find new friends? We resisted the move and even hated the first six months of living in Maryland. But with its economic opportunities and its diverse neighborhoods, Maryland gave us a view of the United States that we had never seen. This transition helped us sever our ties to

Delaware, and it allowed us to sprout new roots where we were. This turn was brought to us, but it would help later when I decided where to go to graduate school and where to live on my own. I was no longer afraid of the changes that accompany moving.

BLUEPRINT

Nothing in life remains the same. If I open my eyes while I am enduring change, I can learn from the trans-formation.

YOUR TESTIMONY

What is the biggest change that has happened in your life in the past six months? Do you like this change? Name several things that are changing in your life. Tell why you like or dislike these changes.

My life has changed by . . .

expression 49

Family members can and will hurt us.

*J*t has been said that the folks who are closest to us hurt us the most. We are bruised the most by the people we love. Our families know things about us that can wound us, and, in the heat of the moment, they say things that they know will hurt.

MY TESTIMONY

While growing up, my brother and I had the typical brother-sister relationship. He wasn't particularly fond of me being around his friends, and I surely didn't want him being around mine. But as I went through personal problems while in college, I didn't have any family to count on except my brother. When things went wrong, I called him. He was the only shoulder that I had to lean on. Then, we'd have bad fights. We'd argue about something really small and then allow it to be blown out of proportion. In our angriest moments, my brother would remind me in a way that hurt me and made me feel bad about myself of the times that I had leaned on him. No verbal exchange has ever hurt me like the ones that I've had with my brother.

BLUEPRINT

Family members can hurt me, but I won't allow that to stop me from moving forward.

YOUR TESTIMONY

When were you hurt by something a family member did or said? Have you ever hurt a family member by doing or saying something?

I was hurt when . . . .

I think I hurt _____ when . . .

expression 50

Popularity can be a burden.

eing a celebrity is when people know you and begin to expect certain things from you. When you're favored, you're expected to be funny, to be successful, to do things at which many other people fail. You're presumed to have a wonderful life. But in the real world it doesn't always work that way. Sometimes it's a struggle to live up to the expectations of our own fame.

MY TESTIMONY

Before my ten-year high school class reunion, I was looking forward to knowing what the most admired kids in my class were now doing. When I was in high school, I had a select group of friends. I was well liked among the people I knew, but I wouldn't exactly have called myself the most popular. There was another group of kids in my school whom everybody knew. They were beloved by the students and the administration. They seemed to have everything going for them. At the reunion, however, many of the most celebrated kids didn't even show up. After I spoke with some fellow classmates, I concluded that those popular kids couldn't face not living up to all of the expectations. Real life had shown them that although they had been well known in high school, that didn't guarantee success in the real world.

BLUEPRINT

I will remember all the times that I wanted to be more popular and that ten years from now, my fame may not get me any bonuses.

YOUR TESTIMONY

What do you think about popularity and people who are popular? Do you consider yourself popular? Why or why not? Do you want to be popular? Why or why not?

I think popularity is . . .

expression 51

Understand the essence of catfights.

*W*omen embroiled in a fight over a boyfriend must be one of the most ridiculous sights to see. The women are angry because of something that a guy did or said. But why aren't the women mad at the man? Most times, he is in the middle, and it's his fault that the two women are fighting. Women don't have time to fight over men.

MY TESTIMONY

My friend Andrea knew a guy in her school who wanted to meet me. According to Andrea, Will was real nice. One night there was a party in town and he asked if I was going. I went with some of my girlfriends and ended up seeing him at the party and he seemed cool. He asked me how I got to the party and offered to give me a ride home. I told him that I had ridden with my friends and that I didn't need a ride. But he insisted and said, "It's on my way, and I'll get to talk to you." Well, when I got to his car, this girl came out from nowhere and told me to get in the back. To my knowledge, it wasn't her car, and I wasn't getting into the back. I looked at Will so that he would explain what was going on. Well, when I looked over at him, this girl, who happened to be his ex-girlfriend—or current girlfriend—grabbed me by the back of my hair. A fight ensued. Before I even realized what was happening, this girl had attacked me because I had accepted a ride from someone who begged me to go with him. It didn't make sense to me. So I never, ever spoke to Will again.

BLUEPRINT

I will not allow myself to fight over men. A man who wants me to fight over him isn't worth my time.

YOUR TESTIMONY

Which girls have you heard about who have fought over a guy? What did you think about their fighting? After two girls fight over a guy, who gets him? Name three reasons why you wouldn't fight over a guy.

expression 52

Know how to love yourself.

Some people feel good when they read a book. Some enjoy buying new jeans or just going shopping. Others find pleasure in doing outside activities. These things that we do are ways of loving ourselves.

MY TESTIMONY

I love nail polish. I love neat-looking hands. When I was growing up my mom had a manicure kit and she would allow me to polish her fingernails. I'd pretend to be a manicurist. I thoroughly enjoyed doing it. Now that I'm older, I enjoy painting my nails. I like looking down at my hands and seeing shades of yellow or purple or blue. Whenever I paint my nails or pick out a new polish, it reminds me of the fun times that I've had with my mom. Seeing all the colors on my fingers represents both hope and happiness. Painting my nails is a simple way to tap into my past and bring pleasure to my present.

BLUEPRINT

I know what makes me feel good about myself, and I will take some time to reflect on the happiest times in my life and remember what I was doing during these times.

YOUR TESTIMONY

What do you love doing for yourself? Why do you love doing these things? Name three things.

Bad things happen to good people.

$\mathcal{W}$hen a devout Christian student gets shot down in broad daylight for not denouncing her belief in God, you know that bad things happen to good people. When an elderly grandmother who is devoted to her grandchildren is set on fire after gently disciplining her grandchild, you know bad things happen to good people.

MY TESTIMONY

A classmate, Gary Johnson, died when he was sixteen. As he was coming home from a high school homecoming party, a tractor trailer crossed lanes and hit him head-on. He died instantly. I campaigned against Gary in our eighth-grade vice presidential election. When I won, he accepted his defeat graciously. He was a nice guy. He was liked by most everyone. He could best be described as a quiet young man with a lot of friends. Our high school mourned his death for a long time. No one could understand why Gary had to die on that day or in that way.

BLUEPRINT

I understand that when good people are taken from this life, they are going to a better place.

YOUR TESTIMONY

What bad things have happened to good people you know? How did it make you feel when you found out?

expression 54

Bad things will happen.

J used to believe that, because of all the bad things that used to happen in my life, God was picking on me. The unfortunate things that would occur, I could hardly explain. Today when I look back at some of my unpleasant experiences, I regard all them, good and bad, as having prepared me to become a better person.

MY TESTIMONY

Veletta, the toughest girl in middle school, didn't like me. One day I was in the cafeteria and I happened to look over at her. I didn't know who she was. She was wearing a tacky bright-colored outfit. I mentioned to one of my friends that I didn't particularly like the colors and then changed the subject. Well, that "friend" happened to be Veletta's cousin. She told Veletta what I had said about her outfit. I wasn't trying to be mean, but Veletta came after me because I had talked about her. For weeks, I dreaded going to school because I was told repeatedly that Veletta was going to beat me up on sight. The comment that I made about her outfit was mild compared to being pummeled. I couldn't figure out what I had done to deserve the threats that hung over my head for weeks or the nightmares that accompanied them. Perhaps the lesson was this: Don't talk about people unless you're prepared for the consequences.

BLUEPRINT

Unpleasant occurrences will make me appreciate the good things all the more and I will grow as a result of the turbulence in my life.

YOUR TESTIMONY

Name three bad things that happened in your life. What did you learn as a result of these things?

I learned _____ when _____ happened.

expression 55

Learn from the experiences of others.

$\mathcal{W}$e can learn so much from other people's trials. In gaining knowledge from others, we can witness the pain of the lesson, but not personally feel the anguish of the experience.

MY TESTIMONY

When I was in college, a friend Lana was frantic when she contracted a venereal disease. She immediately called her various sexual partners and asked each if he had infected her. Of course, none of her partners would admit that he had spread the disease to her. I learned so much from her experience. Although I didn't personally go through it, her despair from not knowing who had given her the contagion, and the fact that she had become infected, was enough for me. From Lana's tribulation, I learned that I didn't want to have multiple sexual partners and I didn't want to risk disease by allowing my partner not to wear a condom.

BLUEPRINT

I can be enriched by learning from the experiences of others.

YOUR TESTIMONY

Think about your family and friends. Name three life lessons that you've learned from their experiences.

I learned _____ from _____.

expression 56

Try new things.

You'll never know what you can do until you make an effort. You won't know how far you can reach until you place a bar just beyond your grasp. It's easy to get caught up in everyday life.

MY TESTIMONY

I didn't know how to direct a play or skit when I volunteered to direct a theatrical performance at Morehead State University. I didn't have any expertise in directing actors. My desire to be successful directing this skit allowed me to obtain all the necessary knowledge. The performances were well received, and I learned that although I had known nothing about what I wanted to do, I could learn what I had to know by trying.

BLUEPRINT

Attempting something fresh gives me something to look forward to. I will try different things for myself and see the excitement in my life change.

YOUR TESTIMONY

What would you try if you had more courage? What can you do to feel more comfortable about this endeavor? Jot down ways that could lead you to trying this new thing.

expression **57**

You won't understand everything.

$\mathcal{W}$e think that we must grasp people's actions, their reactions, the whys, whos, and how comes, but there are some things in life that we'll never fully understand.

MY TESTIMONY

Just after I turned eighteen and was being trained in college to ask questions about life, I really began to drill my mom. Anything that she did or said that I didn't completely accept, I challenged. Before long, my inquiries created a certain amount of tension. In my mind, I had to have answers, but my mom was simply tired of my wisecracks. I sensed that a wedge had formed between us and knew that if I didn't cut back on some of my probing, my mom probably wouldn't want to talk to me much at all. I learned then that I had to let go of some of the things that I didn't understand.

BLUEPRINT

I know that I won't understand everything. For the things that I don't understand, I will find the strength to let them go.

YOUR TESTIMONY

Name three situations that you didn't understand that involved your mother, your best friend, or one of your cousins.

I didn't understand when Mom . . .

expression 58

You will experience heartbreak.

The pain that comes from being in love is necessary for our individual growth. Heartache teaches us the depth of personal interactions. People who give themselves to the chance of love live in a freer, less guarded existence.

MY TESTIMONY

I fell in love hard my junior year in college. Cal pursued me aggressively and showered me with attention. I was hesitant to begin dating him, but his persistence wore me down. We enjoyed each other's company and were very compatible. About a year into the relationship, I sensed that he was cheating. A couple of months later, I visited his house and saw a big Valentine's Day card for him that I hadn't bought. My stomach hurt, my heart hurt, my head hurt, and my ears were ringing. In fact, I got an instant case of diarrhea. My heart had never been broken like that before.

BLUEPRINT

I will allow myself to experience love. It's one of God's greatest treasures.

YOUR TESTIMONY

How did you know your heart was broken? What did it feel like it?

I was heartbroken when . . .

expression 59

Know the signs and report date rape.

*D*ate rape means being sexually violated by someone you know during an outing or get-together. There might have been a time when you could be on a date and "no" meant "get off me." Then came a time when you would say no and the guy would act like he didn't hear you or didn't understand what you were saying. That's the time that many of us live in now. Because the rapist is not a stranger, women are often unsure if what they experienced was actually rape. Well, if someone you know overpowers you and forces you to have sex against your will, that's rape. Report it.

MY TESTIMONY

The first time that I ever had sex, I was raped. The guy was bigger than me, he was stronger than me, and he took advantage of me. I was so young and so naive, I couldn't even comprehend what had happened. Things occurred so fast, and sex was so far from my mind, I didn't know what was going on. Now, many years later,

I understand. And now I know rape is occurring in epidemic proportions to young women.

BLUEPRINT

I have to report date rape because if I don't, the guy will continue to hurt other women.

YOUR TESTIMONY

Why is being forced to have sex a terrible thing? What would you do if you were facing that situation?

If I were in that situation I would . . .

Your mother was a little girl once.

$\mathcal{W}$hen you realize that your mother was somebody's child who grew up and had a family of her own, your heart will probably break. For some reason we just want to believe that our mom was put on the earth the minute we were born. Sometimes it's difficult to realize that she has a life separate from ours.

MY TESTIMONY

I guess I would never have allowed my mother to have a life if she and my father had not gotten divorced. As a family, my mother and father belonged to me and my brother. But once my parents got divorced and my mom began dating, it seemed that I no longer had influence over her life. She decided to be an independent woman who could go on dates, go shopping, and make her own decisions, whether her children agreed with her or not. Accepting my mother as an individual apart from myself has been the hardest part of being an adult child. But my mom is also Bertha's daughter, and Bertha's daughter grew up with dreams of her own, and her dreams were born long before I was.

BLUEPRINT

I will accept my mother for who she is and love her for what she's done. I realize that she has her own life.

YOUR TESTIMONY

Ask your mother about what her life was like when she was thirteen. Talk to your mother about what she liked most about school. Write down some of the things that she tells you.

Understand the need for respect.

*M*any people misunderstand respect. Some think it is bowing down to others. That's why so many have problems giving folks deference. Respect is knowing someone's contributions and acknowledging them. It's appreciation for the road that someone else built so that we may travel. Respect, like reverence, is identifying with the building blocks of a situation and paying homage to their existence.

MY TESTIMONY

I had a professor at Hampton University who was the first black woman to receive a Ph.D. in sociology from the University of California at Berkeley. I took many of her classes. She never bragged about her accomplishments, but she always spoke from her knowledge pool. When I thought about attending graduate school and needed to talk to someone about it, I knew she was the person with whom to speak. At least twenty years had passed between her entrance to graduate school and when I first entered, but I respected her knowledge about the new situation that I was entering.

BLUEPRINT

I am not so grand in my individuality that I cannot respect those who came before me. I will offer my recognition to others.

YOUR TESTIMONY

Who do you have the most respect for who isn't related to you? Why do you respect that person so much?

I respect _____ because . . .

expression 62

Sometimes you'll have to start over.

Staying in a dire predicament prevents us from partici-
pating in the next level of joy in our lives. God does not
want us to suffer. So when we do, He wants us to find our
way out of it. But to end the misery, sometimes we must
begin again and again and again.

MY TESTIMONY

I had been in a negative relationship for a long time. I
often felt that I could not breathe. I remained in it
because I believed that it was easier to stay than it was
to leave. I wasted many months of personal happiness.
The day that I decided to leave, I felt that a five-
hundred-pound anchor had been released from my
body. I wasn't excited about beginning my love life all
over, but I was excited about being freer and lighter.
Later, I became excited about my new life.

BLUEPRINT

Each time that I start over, I am getting a newer, fresher lease on life. I will not be afraid to begin again.

YOUR TESTIMONY

Have you ever moved into a new neighborhood, gone to a new school, made new friends? What was it like for you to start over? Was it as bad as you thought? Was it better?

expression 63

Ignore insults.

$\mathcal{W}$ords can be painful, but our decision to dwell on insults is often more painful than the words themselves. You have no control over the negative things that people will say about you.

MY TESTIMONY

I can remember being ridiculed in my childhood. I recall someone telling me that my teeth weren't straight or that my hair wasn't long enough or that my skin wasn't light enough. Those taunts bothered me when I was twelve years old and maybe even when I was fifteen. By the time I turned nineteen, those kinds of insults didn't affect me much, if at all.

BLUEPRINT

I control my mind and how I think about myself. I will not be distracted by the painful words of others.

YOUR TESTIMONY

What are the most negative insults that have been said to you? How did you deal with them?

I was told _____.

expression 64

Being mean is often a front for something else.

*T*here are people who are mad at the summer for being hot, who are similarly mad at winter for being cold. Some folks don't like anybody or anything. There are those who just go through life being evil to others as if nice was a foreign country that they don't want to visit. Cruelty and anger are such a waste of energy. Oftentimes people use meanness as a way to reach out to us.

MY TESTIMONY

I had a relative who used to be mean to everybody. If you spoke to her at a family reunion she'd growl at you instead of saying hello. The family nonchalantly regarded her manners as "just the way she is." Over the years, no one in the extended family really tried to be close to her. Most of us felt she was just too spiteful. Now that we're all older, we've learned that she was the victim of child molestation. She wasn't really trying to be irascible, she was trying to give the family clues that she wasn't okay. And instead of any of us figuring out why she was so ornery, we elected not to reach out to her at all. Now, years later, we all regret not having paid attention to the signs that she was giving us.

BLUEPRINT

I shouldn't readily discard people who are unkind; instead I should reach out to them to see if I can uncover the origin.

YOUR TESTIMONY

Are you mean at certain times or on specific occasions? Do certain cues in your life spark you to become mean?

I get mean when . . .

expression 65

Make the best use of your time.

I might not have as much time as you to make it to the finish line, but as fast as I'm going, I'll get there just the same. Sometimes when I think about people whose lives have ended while they were in their prime, I feel like crying. Often, I get fed up because I know they could have done more if they had had more time. As sad as I become about people who have lost their lives in their twenties, thirties, or forties, I should be equally saddened by the people who live to their nineties yet do not accomplish what they have dreamed.

MY TESTIMONY

If my heart were to stop beating as I prepare this manuscript, I would be okay with death. Someone could come to my computer, get the ideas, and take them to a publisher. My life would have ended while I was doing something that I love to do. Every day of my life I spend doing what I like to do. I'm not going to wait until I'm fifty and half my life is over to decide what makes me happy. I enjoy making progress every day. The race is on. If you're not already running, you better get started.

BLUEPRINT

One life is all I have, and the way I use it is how I show how important my life is to me. I will make better use of my time.

YOUR TESTIMONY

What are five things that you need to do but you haven't done? Why are you procrastinating?

I need to . . .

expression 66

Don't be afraid to disagree.

$\mathcal{W}$hen you begin to see life as it actually is and not how people have presented it to you, you may become argumentative. Not accepting the status quo can be an unsettling thing for some people.

MY TESTIMONY

The conversations that I had with my father changed drastically when I became an adult. Around my twenty-first birthday, I remember thinking, I'm not gonna sit here and agree with everything you say. Maybe I did that for the first twenty-one years of my life, when I wasn't sure of my opinion, but now? No way! I have my own opinions. My father is the type of person who will talk to you all day about an opinion, especially if you agree with him. I don't dislike my father because I often clash with him, but I do argue with him because some of my thoughts are different from his.

BLUEPRINT

I will be courageous in sharing my opinion with others. I won't concern myself with whether someone agrees with me.

YOUR TESTIMONY

Consider your home and school life. What are some practices or policies at these places that you disagree with? Why do you disagree?

At home, I disagree with . . .

expression 67

Know that hate still exists.

$\mathcal{P}$eople still hate other people because of their differences, and in some cases because of their similarities. Everybody isn't like that, but haters do exist. Keep your heart and your eyes open.

MY TESTIMONY

Imagine being fresh out of college, feeling empowered about your recent accomplishment. You, along with your family, head to Lake Tahoe, Nevada, for a vacation. You stop at a bright tourist location to buy some water. It's hot as a Mexico summer. As you're patiently waiting in line, the cashier looks at you, then looks around you to help the white gentleman standing behind you. The cashier chose not to wait on you. Just like that, instead of feeling empowered, you feel dirty, you feel grimy. You think something is wrong with you. It happened to me on my first vacation after graduating from college.

BLUEPRINT

I will not allow hate to stop me. I will get to know, communicate, and have honest relationships with people of all races, creeds, and colors.

YOUR TESTIMONY

People are hated for many reasons. Name three. Do you hate anyone? Why or why not?

expression 68

Learn to work it out.

$\mathcal{T}$hings aren't always going to go as planned, but we have to learn how to make them work. It seems that when love relationships begin to get rocky, the first thing people want to do is leave. The last thing they want to do is communicate. When a professor doesn't get the message across to students effectively, the first thing that the students want to do is drop the class rather than seek out the professor for additional instruction.

MY TESTIMONY

As a freshman, I chose art appreciation as my liberal arts elective. At the time, I thought the class would be easy. I went every day, and then when we would have tests, I'd find myself completely stumped. When I tried to talk to the professor, I still didn't understand the material. I started showing up to class late, then every other class period. When I took subsequent tests, I was even more confused than I had been before. I gave up on trying to talk to the professor. I gave up on the class. In fact, I didn't even take the final examination. Well, I got an F in the class. Three years later, as a senior, I had to take another liberal arts class because I hadn't successfully passed my freshman elective. I still didn't appreciate that art class, but at least I didn't fail it.

BLUEPRINT

Running away from a situation is not solving it. I will work out my challenges through communication and effort.

YOUR TESTIMONY

What existing problem do you need to work out? Why haven't you worked it out? Why would it be good for you to resolve this problem?

I need to resolve a problem that I have with . . .

expression **69**

Don't waste time on self-indulgence.

*B*e proud, but do not let pride stop you from going forward. You can take a moment to pat yourself on the back, but don't turn that moment into an hour of gloating and self-indulgence. We can be proud of what we do in our lives, but don't become too proud that you forget what your goals are or what your purpose is.

MY TESTIMONY

I remember times after I had started my magazine when I would still go out and drop off issues at various college campuses. Some of the students who saw me couldn't believe that I owned a publication and had done a motivational tour, yet still would go out on the campus and drop off copies. If there was something that my company required, I could never be too too proud to get it done. In the end, my goal was to reach the students. It didn't matter if I dropped off the magazines or someone else did. I refused to allow egoism to get in the way of my purpose.

BLUEPRINT

No matter how happy I am to get to a certain point in my life, work still has to be done. I will not allow pride to get in the way of my work.

YOUR TESTIMONY

Have you recently spent too much time being selfish? Name three people who have helped you become a better person. They may be relatives, people from school, church, summer programs, etc.

_____ *helped me when she . . .*

expression 70

Unplanned pregnancies are not all by accident.

$\mathcal{U}$nintended pregnancies have become commonplace. So have the claims that they occur by accident. But if we have sex and don't protect ourselves, admittedly or not, we have planned for a pregnancy.

MY TESTIMONY

I remember one of my associates telling me she was pregnant. She hadn't used any birth control and didn't want to have a child, but the pregnancy sort of happened. She knew that she wasn't prepared to have a child and she knew that she wasn't in a significant relationship with the father, but she continued to call the pregnancy an accident. Years later, now that she's had the child and the relationship with the father has all but deteriorated, she is miserable, resentful, and completely unhappy. That planned accident has turned her world upside down.

BLUEPRINT

If I don't plan to prevent it, I plan to make it happen. I will strategize my life plans to maximize my outcomes.

YOUR TESTIMONY

Talk to at least two people who have had children who weren't planned. Ask them how their lives changed when they had kids. Write down what they say. How could your dreams and life change if you had an unplanned pregnancy?

expression 71

Understand how alcohol can make you feel.

Society has a tendency to truly downplay the effects of drinking until one becomes addicted. Alcohol is often introduced to us via fun, entertaining beer commercials. Social drinking is shown on television and film as if only good things occur when we're drinking.

MY TESTIMONY

The last time that I drank alcohol, I was a freshman in college, under the age of twenty-one and about to go to a party at Temple University. I had a couple of wine coolers and I tasted a strawberry daiquiri for the first time. I got in my best friend's car and attempted to drive thirty-five minutes to Philadelphia. Within the first five minutes of the drive, I found myself spinning 360 degrees on a wet bridge, wondering if the car was going to go over the edge. I had four people in the car with me. If it weren't for their weight, I think that car would have gone over the bridge. That day, I swore off drinking.

BLUEPRINT

I will understand blood alcohol levels, drinking under the influence, and when to say when.

YOUR TESTIMONY

What do you know about alcohol? Do a search on the Internet for "women and alcohol." Write down three facts that you learn.

expression 72

Find out who you are.

*a*sk yourself: Do you like being in crowds? Do you like talking to strangers? Are you offended by obscene behavior? Every day we thrust ourselves into circumstances that end up making us feel uncomfortable, yet we never know why. We don't know why because we have never looked into our inner mirrors and asked ourselves who we truly are. Ask yourself who you are.

MY TESTIMONY

Lisa, my housemate during my junior year of college, was from New Jersey and was very outgoing. If she heard about a party, she couldn't wait to get there. On Fridays when I was in the house, unwinding from a week of school, Lisa was figuring out what she was going to wear to that night's party. Lisa loved to hang. I would always become quiet around the house and become antisocial, because I knew in the back of my mind that Lisa would soon ask if I wanted to go out. And, instead of being able to say, "No, I don't like hanging every Friday night," I created an alter-personality that served to push Lisa away. After a couple of months, Lisa and I didn't hang much anymore, and our friendship didn't seem as strong. It wasn't because I didn't like Lisa, it was because I wasn't comfortable telling her who I really was.

BLUEPRINT

I will take the time to find out who I am so that I know when and with whom I am the most comfortable.

YOUR TESTIMONY

What are three distinct parts of your personality that make you different from other people? What do you like most about you?

I'm different because . . .

expression 73

Embrace new friendships.

$\mathcal{T}$he friends you've known since childhood may give you the oldest sense of yourself, but new friends add depth to your character and allow you to experience trust at new heights.

MY TESTIMONY

I have a friend named Veronica whom I met in college. She grew up in Texas. Having grown up in Delaware, I had never known anybody from Texas. Meeting Veronica was like a breath of fresh air; I didn't know anyone like her. She was so self-confident, full of energy, and striking looking, all of which you sensed in the first fifteen seconds of meeting her. She was that kind of person. When we first met, I don't know what it was about her that made me like her. As I reflect, I remember that she had an easygoing manner, but really she's the kind of friend who makes looking good seem effortless. I call it her God-given talent. As Veronica and I became friends, I began to learn more about personal appearance and elegance. I learned about first impressions, but more important, I learned about the essential first fifteen seconds. My new friendship with Veronica opened my eyes to a new way of looking at fashion.

BLUEPRINT

I will embrace new friendships. New friends who can expand my view of the world while also challenging me to trust myself are definitely worth getting to know.

YOUR TESTIMONY

Is there anyone who you've met recently who you would like to consider a friend? What do you believe that you like about that person? Why would you like to have some new friends?

I met _____ . . .

expression 74

Be encouraged to take on new challenges.

*B*eing in a new environment away from parents allows us to make independent decisions. There are challenges that we face away from Mom that we must learn how to handle on our own.

MY TESTIMONY

Every time that I overcharged my credit card, I called my mom so that she would help me make my monthly payment. When I spent more money on summer clothes than I saved for textbooks, I called my mom so that she would help me out. Sometimes when I would call and ask for her help, my mom would seemingly grunt on the phone. She grew tired of hearing me ask for the things that I should have been able to budget for myself. Every time I heard her disapproving sounds, it was like I was ten years old again, asking for twenty-five cents to buy a candy bar. I took the hints from my mom. As I began to ask for less and less, I began to feel more and more like a real adult.

BLUEPRINT

I will resist the urge to ask my parents or guardians how to handle all of my new challenges. The best part of some of my challenges is being able to face and conquer them by myself.

YOUR TESTIMONY

What challenge have you recently faced that you wished that you didn't have to go to your mother or an older person about? Why did you go to her? Do you think you'll be able to handle that situation soon on your own?

PHASE 3

Fortification

FORTIFICATION—Your fortification strengthens your life and reinforces decisions and experiences that empower, motivate, and encourage you in your journey through womanhood with the purpose of making you a strong woman.

expression 75

Resist behavior that sabotages your goals.

$\mathcal{I}$t seems that some of us are into self-sabotage. We know that doing certain things will cause us problems, but we do them anyway. Why do we engage in certain behaviors knowing that they will affect us negatively?

MY TESTIMONY

I remember going to job interviews and habitually being late to almost all of them. I would go with the ready-made excuse "I didn't know where the office was." My tardiness never made a good impression on my would-be employers, but I was too busy in self-sabotage to even notice. I have to admit that I've probably not been hired for a couple of jobs because of showing up late to the interview. Now, that's sad. I needed those jobs. I could have looked for the locations earlier, but I just didn't do that. I apparently wanted to hurt myself more than I wanted to succeed.

BLUEPRINT

I will avoid behaviors that hurt me.

YOUR TESTIMONY

What act have you engaged in that caused you to hurt yourself? Why did you do it in the first place? After you realized that you hurt yourself, how did you feel?

I hurt myself when . . .

expression 76

Know the importance of molding your life.

There aren't many athletes who are afraid of a workout. Few scientists refuse to touch a microscope. All doctors must study the body before doing an operation. Athletes, scientists, and doctors alike realize the need to shape their lives to fit their respective goals.

MY TESTIMONY

When I was in college, particularly in my junior and senior years, I wanted to be a straight-A student. I had been distracted significantly during my first two years, so it was now time for me to buckle down. As much as I had identified with wanting to get good grades, I did not have any of the habits that the smart students had. I didn't know how to utilize my time for studying or understand the bonus of teachers' office hours. I didn't realize the significance of study groups. Once I became committed to studying hard, I molded my life to participate in the habits that other good students had. I learned how to study and I took advantage of study groups. It was habit-changing and habit-forming, but I did it. I became the person I desired to be.

BLUEPRINT

In making my dreams a reality, I have to be willing to mold my life to achieve the desired results.

YOUR TESTIMONY

Is there a person who does something that you may want to do when you grow up? Ask that person how she got started and what she did to become successful. Write down some of the things that she did.

expression 77

Notice your individual growth.

*W*hat were you doing five years ago? What do you anticipate doing five years from now? Whatever stage you are in, recognize the realities of growth.

MY TESTIMONY

I had no idea what career I would choose when I entered my university with an undeclared major. At the end of my first year, I chose journalism as my major. Then as I entered my second year, I became a sociology major. Each time I thought I was secure about my education specialty, an inner voice told me to go in another direction. At those times, it was daunting to think I didn't know what vocation to select. I realize now that every step I made, whether to the right or left, was a step toward me growing.

BLUEPRINT

I realize that if I am not doing the same thing, the same way, then I am growing. Each day contains a potential for growth. I will take advantage of it.

YOUR TESTIMONY

What are you doing now that you weren't doing three years ago? What will you be doing three years from now that you aren't doing today? Why are you happy about your growth?

I'm happy with . . .

expression 78

Condoms are not too small.

*M*any men have said, "Baby, I can't fit into a condom. They're too small." Men wish they were so special that they could put prophylactic manufacturers out of business. But the truth is, the average man and the above-average man can fit into a condom. If you run into a guy who just believes that no rubber can fit his mammoth size, go to the pharmacist and ask for the largest condoms ever made. And when your man tells you he can't fit one, whip out your supply.

MY TESTIMONY

I remember in health education class some wise guy telling the teacher that condoms aren't for everybody. The same guy told the class that he couldn't even fit into one. Some of the girls in class laughed, but I looked at him like he was crazy. I found it hard to believe that rubbers weren't being made to fit every size. Our health educator informed the class that the smart aleck was like many men who want their girlfriends to believe that they couldn't fit into prophylactics. But they actually can.

BLUEPRINT

I will not believe the guy who tells me that he cannot fit into a condom.

YOUR TESTIMONY

Search the Internet; learn about condoms. Write down three things that you learned about condoms that you didn't know before.

Condoms are . . .

expression 79

Appreciate the strength of your life story.

If someone were writing a book on your life, would they be fascinated by how you've changed? In thumbing through your family album, perhaps there would be a picture of you with no teeth, then a picture of you with baby teeth, maybe even a picture of you with braces. Anybody looking at the photos would see how you've developed. In adulthood the growth isn't always as easily shown in photographs: but it is evident. As you get older, realize that your life story continues to change.

MY TESTIMONY

In grade school, I wasn't really comfortable standing up for myself. I had grown up in a household where I didn't have to. In middle school, I became comfortable with my presence and the power that I could wield over people. In high school, I became confused by peer pressure and teenage situations, and, as a result, I acted out using violence and curse words. By the time I graduated from college, I knew exactly who I was and what that meant to me and to other people as well. Understanding my personal story gave me great confidence.

BLUEPRINT

I will not beat myself up for not running as fast as I could have on some days. I will be encouraged in knowing that I've been making progress all along.

YOUR TESTIMONY

Write a short story about your life. You're the star. Your name is in lights.

expression 80

Never accept a label for women that you're not comfortable with.

_W_omen must be held in high regard for what they bring to the world. With the acceptance of "bitch," "ho," and "baby mama" labels, the esteem for women has been brought to an all-time low. We have always been and will always be the creators of the earth, the teachers, and the nurturers.

MY TESTIMONY

When the group HWA (Hoez With Attitude) came out with an album sporting the "Yeah, I'm a ho. Where's my money?" attitude, the general perception of black women took a hit. It wasn't that every woman subscribed to the philosophy that they were hos, it was the fact that HWA sent out the shock wave that certain women were willing to call themselves Hoez With Attitude for money. Many thought there must be more hos out there. Men began to look at women on the street and say, "Okay, she's a ho, she's a ho, she's a ho." Ho became a common association for every woman. Tell me the last time you heard a woman being called a "ho" or "bitch" in public and it made you feel good? When?

BLUEPRINT

I won't accept a label that does not make me feel good.

YOUR TESTIMONY

What names have you heard women being called on the radio, on television, and in movies? Which ones didn't you like? Why?

expression 81

Realize when it's time to move on.

*T*here comes a period in our lives—maybe it's between high school and our first real job, or the span when we become adults while in college—when we realize that we should guide the fate of our lives. In this precious moment, we should take note of the direction in which our lives and the lives of our closest friends and associates are going. We may be put in the position to reevaluate the role certain people have in our lives.

MY TESTIMONY

Early in my twenties, having just graduated from Hampton University, I made an assessment of myself and my inner circle. At this point, I discarded an old friendship because I believed that her values and morals had sharply declined from those we shared in childhood. I decided against keeping the communication alive because I didn't want her principles to affect mine. I just faded to black. Today, I am glad that I made that decision because as I continue to grow, I always find myself making value judgments. I read stories time and again about how people have been brought down to their lowest point by those who they thought were their friends.

BLUEPRINT

I will take note of those around me and my influences and will move on accordingly.

YOUR TESTIMONY

Do I have friends in my life whose values I don't agree with? Who are they? How are their values different from mine?

My friend . . .

expression 82

Only you can determine your self-worth.

The way to feel truly good about your accomplishments is through your own hard work. You can't cut corners, you can't let someone else do the job for you. Self-worth grows as you continue to build it through your own efforts.

MY TESTIMONY

I remember a girl in my sociology class who cheated on every test. She felt that as long as she didn't get caught, there was no real point in studying. This classmate didn't think that anyone really cared about the kind of person she was. She thought they only cared about her grades. She aspired to attend graduate school but she didn't believe that she would be accepted without cheating. I don't know what happened to that girl, but I bet she isn't up for a Pulitzer prize or anything. Most likely, she'll never save anyone's life, nor will she be a good role model. Her dishonest efforts undermined her self-confidence and robbed her of her own self-worth.

BLUEPRINT

Good or bad, ultimately, I am the sum of all of my work.

YOUR TESTIMONY

If you were to put a dollar amount on yourself, how much would it be? Why that particular amount? What could you do to make yourself feel that you are worth more?

I'm worth . . .

Never accept "bitch" as a term of endearment.

The nineties ushered in a generation of women who proudly accepted the label "bitch." They define bitches as women who are powerful, who are in control, and who are doing things in their lives. So instead of viewing the word "bitch" as one that weakens, some women look at it as an empowering, endearing term. Unfortunately, a lot of negative energy still accompanies the word.

MY TESTIMONY

One of the most influential executives in urban fashion is a woman. In sharing her own story, Maiza often talks about discrimination, personal trials, and triumphs. When she first entered the business, she wasn't taken seriously and had to make every effort to stand out in a male-dominated industry. Her toughness garnered her success, but it took away some of her inner joy. She often refers to herself as "being bitchy" or mentions that people view her as a bitch. Admittedly, she finds being labeled a bitch strange because when she started out on her journey that was certainly not one of her goals.

BLUEPRINT

I will not allow anyone to refer to me or my sisters as bitches. A word born out of negativity cannot be made positive.

YOUR TESTIMONY

Have you ever been referred to as a bitch? How did you feel? What do yu like or dislike about the word "bitch"?

I was called . . .

expression 84

There will be people who want to take advantage of you.

The less that you know, the more that people will tell you and you will likely believe. Perhaps we do not need advanced degrees in every aspect of life in order not to be taken in by charlatans. We do at least need to be knowledgeable about our own affairs. If someone is trying to tell you more about yourself than you know, then you're going to have problems.

MY TESTIMONY

Having interviewed hundreds of musical artists over the years, I have begun to understand how many of them are bankrupt by the end of their career. I used to be like many people who wondered how musicians end up broke, but understanding belly-up celebrities is not that difficult if you can comprehend their ignorance. These performers rely on others to handle all of their affairs, especially their monetary ones. Trusting individuals who shouldn't be trusted with the heart of their financial stability, these entertainers elect to be in the dark about their economic affairs. Thus, they are often taken advantage of. It's that simple.

BLUEPRINT

I will be knowledgeable on subjects that affect me. I will do my homework so that I won't become easy prey to people who will tell me anything.

YOUR TESTIMONY

When do you feel that you were taken advantage of? What did you do?

I felt I was taken advantage of when . . .

expression 85

No matter how negative the situation, something positive is bound to happen.

*Y*ou've probably heard someone tell you a million times, "Don't let negative people get you down." Many old wives' tales say, "What goes around comes around. Bad people get it in the end." But when you're in the midst of a negative storm, you might find it hard to believe that something positive will happen soon or that your nemesis will someday be worse off than you.

MY TESTIMONY

I remember one of my first jobs out of college. I was working in a team environment and as the administrative support, I had to complete various marketing tasks. As I began to be more proficient, I was on my way to getting a higher position and more money. Then, all of a sudden, all of the coworkers who used to love working with me turned against me and said negative things about my character to my supervisor. The change took place almost overnight, and my coworkers' negative comments affected the raise that I should have received. Instead of feeding into the negativity and being nasty, I allowed the negative storm to pass. Shortly after, positive things occurred. I was able to negotiate for better pay, one of the deceitful coworkers was fired, and life seemed sunny again. Now, when I find myself caught in the middle of negativity, I wait and I'm patient because I know the sun will shine again.

BLUEPRINT

I will be patient. I know something positive is bound to happen.

YOUR TESTIMONY

Name three situations that you thought were negative, but in which something positive happened in the end.

I thought it was bad when . . .

Many paths lead to your dreams.

*I*magine waking up with the idea of what you would like to do with your life. How do you go about reaching your goals? What if one part of you says "travel the world" and the other part says "go to school?" How do you know which path will most likely take you in the right direction? Well, the answer is simple. Many paths lead to your dreams.

MY TESTIMONY

I always had aspirations of being a writer. It didn't matter what kind. At a young age I started composing poetry. When I was twenty-one, I had a vision of becoming a Hollywood screenwriter. Eventually, before I was twenty-five, I was a magazine journalist. But when I graduated from college, I found myself submitting scripts for popular television series. The first Hollywood executive who turned my work down caused me to examine what I should do with my life. It made me question if I was a scribe at all. One rejection, and I jumped off the track. I didn't challenge this Hollywood executive, I just assumed that he was right and went on to something else. I should have challenged him and I should have continued submitting scripts until every secretary in Tinseltown knew me by my first name. I didn't do that. I allowed a little bit of rejection and a whole lot of fear to take hold of me and to take control of my life. But the worst part of all was I had abandoned my dream.

BLUEPRINT

Even in the face of rejection, I will remember my goals. I know that there is no wrong way to attain my aspirations as long as I am earnestly and honestly working toward them. I will remember my dreams always.

YOUR TESTIMONY

What are your dreams? Name three ways to get to them.

expression 87

Don't allow fear to paralyze you.

*W*e are not born with fear. It is something that develops within us and grows with us as we get older. Parents often attempt to instill courage in their children at a young age so that kids will believe that they can do anything. The sight of a child less than three years old swimming in five feet of water, never thinking about her feet not touching the bottom, is daunting to people who refuse to get in water that is over their heads.

MY TESTIMONY

I won't watch gymnastics on television. Seeing the girls maneuver on the parallel bars and the balance beams puts me on the edge of my seat. Thinking about them doing back flips on the beams gives me chills. I recall my days doing cartwheels and headstands on the wooden rail, and I find myself amazed. When I remember dismounts from the parallel bars that I did in my youth, I can hardly believe it. I was that same gymnast that I shudder to see today. I was enrolled in gymnastics and swimming classes before I was introduced to phobias. I did somersaults from the diving platform into ten feet of water before I was aware of the possibility of drowning. My parents were instilling boldness in me before I knew trepidation. I guess they knew that if I was afraid of nothing, I could accomplish anything.

BLUEPRINT

I can be triumphant when I refuse to allow apprehension to enter my mind. I will regain my ability to be fearless.

YOUR TESTIMONY

What are you afraid of? Name three fears that you have and why.

expression 88

You can't keep up the illusion.

There are always pressures to dress a certain way, talk a certain way, or act a certain way. People find comfort in similarities. When the pressure to fit in causes us to act outside of ourselves, we must reconsider.

MY TESTIMONY

I went into debt while attending college trying to dress a certain way to keep up with the wealthiest, most fashionable kids at school. I had to have a new car because the ten-year-old one that I had wasn't hot enough to drive around campus. So, I was faking the funk, trying to keep up with people whom I couldn't keep up with. There is even a real possibility that these college students were fostering an image that wasn't consistent with their reality. Years later, I had to pay the debts incurred while trying to be something that I wasn't. I was a college student who was struggling in school. While my parents and student loans paid for my education, I didn't have the budget to go shopping every week. What a waste of time that was, trying to keep up the façade.

BLUEPRINT

It is not beneficial to me to become something that I am not for the sake of appearances. I will be who I am.

YOUR TESTIMONY

What are some pressures that exist in your school? What do you feel pressured about? What happens when you feel that pressure?

There is pressure to . . .

expression 89

Accept your past.

The secrets we keep about ourselves often eat us from within. We're worried about people finding out about our past and not liking us because of who we used to be.

MY TESTIMONY

One of my best friends from college knows everything about me. While sitting in her dorm room a while back, the feeling overcame me that I should share who I truly am. As I told her about my past, she was saddened to hear of the pain that I endured, but she hugged me and loved me anyway. I knew if Themisa could look at me the same, knowing all the things that I had been through, there was no sense in letting a secret get the best of me. At that point, my history became irrelevant.

BLUEPRINT

I will not allow my past to haunt me. I accept who I am, where I've been, and embrace where I'm going.

YOUR TESTIMONY

What don't you like about your past? Write down how these disliked things cannot stop you from moving forward.

expression 90

Stay in touch with extended family.

As the world becomes more isolated, we must stay in touch with our relatives. We should make it a priority to know what our first, second, and third cousins are doing. We need to know how our aunts and uncles are doing.

MY TESTIMONY

I used to be envious when I heard coworkers talk about how their cousin was a mover and shaker at a firm or their uncle was doing well with entrepreneurship. I silently wondered when my family would begin talking about the successful things that we were doing. Then, I thought maybe my family wasn't flourishing at all; therefore, there was no reason for them to talk. At family reunions, I started connecting with relatives and realized that we were thriving, but we didn't share our achievements with one another.

BLUEPRINT

I will not become a stranger to my family tree. I want to know all of its branches and all of its leaves.

YOUR TESTIMONY

Name five family members who you would like to stay in touch with. How will you get their phone numbers, addresses, or e-mails? Write the contact info here.

expression 91

Be able to sell yourself.

Successful people tend to exude an essence that other people want to be a part of. This aura comes from overcoming obstacles, believing in yourself, and being persistent.

MY TESTIMONY

I never thought that I could sell anything. In fact, I emphatically believed that I could not. When I decided to become an entrepreneur, I had to cast aside any negative thoughts about hustling. I started reading books and subscribing to the power of positive thinking. Time passed and before I even realized it, I was securing advertisements, marketing a magazine, and winning people over in droves. People started to buy what I was offering and I became an effective agent. But more than the advertisements, more than the magazine, I was hawking myself. People believed in my product because they bought into my image and my self-confidence.

BLUEPRINT

If I ever want people to believe in me, I will create an essence of my best qualities and wear it like a tailor-made business suit.

YOUR TESTIMONY

What are your best qualities? How can you make those qualities stand out?

expression **9 2**

Remain persistent and focused.

When you have your eyes set on something—be it a relationship, a new job, or career aspirations—people have a way of distracting you and taking your eyes off your goal. You must remain focused on your objectives.

MY TESTIMONY

I was determined to have the kind of career that I liked. I never wanted to be a person who began to hate my life because I hated my employer. When I graduated from college, I stepped out into the workforce, applying only for jobs that I preferred. I resisted applying for positions I was only interested in for the money. Initially, I didn't make the kind of cash that I desired, but I was never unhappy. I was tenacious and I continued to walk the path leading me to my target.

BLUEPRINT

Even if I get to a certain point and my journey doesn't live up to my expectations, I will stay concentrated on my goals.

YOUR TESTIMONY

What do you want to do with your life? Name three things.

expression **9 3**

Associate yourself with success.

The old slogan "Birds of a feather flock together" is true on many fronts. Successful individuals like to associate with others like them. Similarly, people who are content with doing badly fraternize with folks who share similar predicaments. If you want to soar, you must lift yourself to the occasion and surround yourself with those who think likewise.

MY TESTIMONY

Fresh out of college, there was this guy on television who promised to restore people's credit. He was also a financial whiz. While I was working at an independent financial institution, I got the chance to meet Ryland, and we began a professional relationship. I began working for him part time and he mentored me. A fatherly figure, he had attended Georgetown Law School and had a couple of businesses, and I saw the opportunity to associate myself with him. In the first three months after our meeting, I learned more about personal credit, bank loans, and establishing my personal fortune than I ever thought I'd know. By our association, I increased my knowledge and was a step closer to projecting an effective image.

BLUEPRINT

I can be enhanced by my relationships with prosperous individuals. I will align myself with success and see my life's outlook change.

YOUR TESTIMONY

Name prosperous people in your school, family, or church. How can you work with them to help reach your goals?

expression 94

Be happy about something in your life.

There is always something that you can be cheerful about. People may go through life being unhappy because they didn't get the job that they wanted, all the while forgetting that there are men and women who are unemployed. Some go through life being miserable because their hair isn't long enough, forgetting that others suffer through illnesses that make them completely bald. There are so many aspects of living, and for all the things that make us sorrowful, surely there is one thing that we can be joyous about.

MY TESTIMONY

My parents divorced when I was seventeen years old. When I came home one holiday from college, the house that we had lived in for the past nine years was sold. My mother wanted to get on with her life. My father, who decided to move in with his new love interest, was clearly moving on with his. I was still living in the past.

For many years, I had disliked both of my parents because I felt that they had needlessly destroyed my family. Then, one day, I concluded that I wouldn't carry the anger from my parents' divorce around anymore. I decided that it was good for me to have both of them in my life and I would be grateful for that. And, just like that, I became happy.

BLUEPRINT

I will find something in my life to be happy about, whether it be my personality, my friends, my interests, or my hobbies.

YOUR TESTIMONY

Name ten things about your life that make you happy.

expression 9 5

Don't worry about how, just do.

*P*arents send their children to college without knowing how they're going to pay the tuition. Entrepreneurs start businesses that they don't know how to run, yet they find a way to make them profitable. Sometimes you just have to go forward without full understanding of the process.

MY TESTIMONY

One of the most popular questions that I'm asked when speaking to students about starting a magazine is, "How did you finance it?" Then I'm asked, "Did you go to class to learn how to do it?" When I decided that I was going to have a publication, I focused on what kind. I concentrated on what the result was going to be. In fact, I never really thought about how I was going to finance it or how I was going to do it. If I had thought about those issues, I probably would have been too intimidated to start the enterprise.

BLUEPRINT

I don't have time to worry about how. If I concentrate on doing, I will learn how in the process.

YOUR TESTIMONY

What do you worry about? Name those things.

expression 96

We need peace of mind.

*a*lways allow your conscience to be clear. Be able to sleep at night. Don't let evildoing rob you of your peace. Some people believe that there aren't any real consequences to their wrongdoings. Some believe that they can get away with a heart full of guilt. Let's not kid ourselves.

MY TESTIMONY

Driving my friend's car, I was going fast and got into an accident. Although I realized that the crash was totally my fault, I didn't know how to face Lisa. When I had to tell her about the incident, I didn't feel comfortable being truthful. I blamed the rain. I blamed the bridge. She forgave me, but I worried that our other friends would tell her what really happened. I couldn't sleep peacefully until I told Lisa how recklessly I had driven. The moment that I told her, I felt better. My mind was at ease.

BLUEPRINT

If I strive to live with a clear conscience, I will always have peace of mind.

YOUR TESTIMONY

What is preventing you from having peace of mind? What do you need to be forgiven for? Write statements of forgiveness to address the issues that are preventing you from attaining peace.

I need to be forgiven for . . .

expression 97

Stand united with your family.

*T*he family is our strength. Throughout our lives, families face various crises, but in our trials we must stand together. We have to become more supportive of one another.

MY TESTIMONY

From ages seventeen to twenty-nine, my brother had his share of personal problems. From run-ins with the law and bad-apple friends to outright foolishness, he's experienced a lot. He was the first one in our family to go to college and when he wanted to drop out, my mother was devastated. He always said that he would go back to school, but in the meantime, he would accept dead-end jobs that didn't challenge his intellect. Well, when he turned thirty, he enrolled himself in college, became a straight-A student, and worked full time. My mother and I pitched in to help him buy a computer. We wanted him to know that we believed in him and we supported his efforts. As my brother continues to grow as a person, we're so proud of him and we're so thankful that we didn't give up on him when everything wasn't going well. He's a part of our family and deserving of our support.

BLUEPRINT

I must remember to stand united with my family. I will always be there for my relatives.

YOUR TESTIMONY

Which family members need your support? Name them. Think about ways that you can support them.

expression 98

Deal with the truth.

*H*ow can you be confident about telling people the truth when what they really want is a watered-down version of their reality? How can you be honest when you know that it will hurt someone's feelings? Candor, at times, can be difficult to handle, but the reality is you're either going to deal in facts or you're going to deal in lies. Folks must learn to respect those who speak and act with verity.

MY TESTIMONY

One of my friends loves to think about and reflect on other people's problems. Because of her training, she is the best person to talk to if you're having a personal crisis. But in her life, she can't manage her own dilemmas. When she asks friends to evaluate her obstacles, she doesn't want to hear brutal honesty. She becomes angry and argumentative when she is given the lowdown about her actions. In order to spare her feelings, for many years, I decided to tell her partial truths. Now, years later I've realized that none of those conversations ever helped her to better herself because they weren't dealing with reality.

BLUEPRINT

I don't want the truth to be painful, but it sometimes is. I will have confidence in being honest, and I won't be tempted to lie because I think it will be less painful for somebody.

YOUR TESTIMONY

When were you last struggling to tell somebody the truth? Why was it so hard?

It was hard because . . .

expression **99**

Do it your way.

$\mathcal{T}$imes are always changing. The reason you decide to go to college today is very different from what your decisions will be ten or fifteen years from now. The reason you decide to work at one job today will be different from how you will feel two years from now.

MY TESTIMONY

When I set out to become a writer, I decided that I would get to know people in the entertainment business. Many family members and friends didn't agree with my path toward becoming a journalist. But now that I am a scribe, few doubt my navigating abilities. I couldn't become one doing it in the way of Shakespeare, Maya Angelou, or Mary Higgins Clark. I had to do it the way that I wanted and, ultimately, the way that I felt comfortable.

BLUEPRINT

There is no formula for my life but the one that I create. People on the sidelines may disagree with my course of action, but ultimately, I have to do things my way.

YOUR TESTIMONY

If you were to write about what you want to do with your life, what would you write? Write it now.

I want to do _____ with my life.

Epilogue

$\mathcal{B}$efore you ever picked up this book, I suspect you thought that certain things happened only to you. Hopefully, after reading *The Blueprint for My Girls*, you now realize that I've gone through a lot of the same things. In fact, there are a bunch of girls going through a lot of the same things as you. The key is not to simply go through things but to learn from them and become adept at handling every situation. If you take three things out of this book of ninety-nine expressions, I hope they are: keep a positive outlook, be determined, and realize that you will make mistakes.

As I've grown, I've found that no matter which path I take, there is always going to be a challenge that I must overcome. Life is just like that. But I've made the decision to remain focused on what I want for my life in spite of those challenges. I encourage you to be of like mind. There is a popular saying: "Keep your eyes on the prize." We must do exactly that. No matter how difficult, no matter the challenges, no matter what, stay focused. Know that there is no pain, no problem that lasts forever.

You will make mistakes. We all make mistakes because our decisions can be based only on the knowledge we have at the time. When we don't have complete information or the right information, our decisions end up being bad ones. But that's okay. Mistakes are a part of life—just like breathing. The goal is always to learn from your mistakes. Also, be encouraged by the decisions that you make because that lets you know you're really living!

Right now, you're getting a first taste of what life is gonna be like when you're out on your own. We have to keep going and growing. Entering womanhood is awesome, but the learning, growing, and obstacle facing are not going to stop. As you grow into womanhood, it's going to seem as if the world wants you to be bionic—be stronger, faster, and smarter. The lessons learned from this book are going to keep coming back. My advice to you is to continue to keep a journal of your experiences. Long after you leave young adulthood, writing in a journal will provide the positive reinforcement that you need in your life to strive and thrive.

When I was growing up, I often felt that I didn't have the emotional support that I needed. I did not believe that my family understood where I was coming from or where I wanted to go. The fact that I didn't have someone in my life to tell me and then show me how I could make it brought me great distress. I needed someone to tell me that I could be the best and then point me in the right direction. I needed someone to tell me that I was a leader and then encourage me to lead. I want to let you know that you don't have to wait for a cheerleader. You can do all that you put your mind to. You are strong—strong enough to overcome every obstacle and determined enough to make your dreams come true. In spite of any mistakes you've made, you're still destined to have a meaningful, important life. Enjoy who you are. Enjoy the process of becoming a stronger and better you. This is your life. Love every minute of it. I believe in your power and so should you.

P.S. I often visit schools, churches, and social organizations and talk to girl's groups about the very topics in this book. Tell your friends and group leaders about me and we'll be able to meet in person.

Index

A

abuse, 12, 13, 21–22, 25, 61–62, 69–70
acceptance, 23–24, 37–38, 123, 183–84
actions:
  consequences of, 111–12
  explaining, 69–70
advice, 83–84
alcohol, 145–46
aloneness, 79–80
apologizing, 33–34
aspirations, 77–78, 177–78, 189
attention, craving, 85–86

B

bad things, 109–10, 111–12
bitches, women as, 171–72
burning bridges, 65–66

C

careers, 77–78, 159, 177–78, 189
catfights, 105–6
challenges, 151–52, 205
change, 99–100, 193–94

commitment, 9–10
communication, 93–94, 139, 140
complaints, 11–12
composition, 73
condoms, 161–62
confiding in others, 41–42
criticism, 61–62, 111–12

D

danger, sensing, 3
date rape, 121–22
death, 35–36, 91–92, 109
desertion, 97–98
determination, 205, 206–7
disagreements, 135–36
divorce, 49, 123, 193–94
doing:
  it your way, 203–4
  just, 195–96
  what you say, 9–10

E

ethics, 21–22
excellence, 31–32
expressing yourself, 3–4, 17–18

F

fairness, 89–90
faith, 25–26
family, 83–84, 99–100, 101–2, 131–32, 185–86, 199–200, 206
  See also fathers; mothers; parents; siblings
fathers, 7, 9, 49–50, 135
fear, 179–80
finishing projects, 51–52
focusing, 189–90, 205
fortification, 153
foundation, 1
friends, 39–40, 67–68, 93–94, 149–50, 167–68
frustrations, 87–88

G

getting ahead, 89–90
goals, 60, 155–56, 157–58, 177–78, 189–90, 205
God, 25–26, 127
good people, and bad things, 109–10
gossip, 45–46
growth, 159–60, 205, 206

About the Author

YASMIN SHIRAZ is an empowerment speaker, entertainment journalist, author, and entrepreneur. A graduate of Hampton University and Morehead State University, Shiraz uses her sociology training to empower young people through her books, writings, and speaking engagements.

As an empowerment speaker, she includes among her topics: *The Blueprint for My Girls* empowerment series, transitioning into womanhood, decision-making skills for young people, self-awareness is power, entrepreneurship, and her signature "How to Get into the Entertainment Business" tour. She has spoken at numerous colleges nationwide and has presented her work for sororities, social organizations, political organizations, and the like.

She is perhaps best known as a journalist who has interviewed such celebrities as Sean "P. Diddy" Combs, Jay-Z, Jada Pinkett-Smith, Nas, Queen Latifah, Johnnie Cochran, Lil' Kim, Martin Lawrence, Brandy, and others. For many years she owned the most successful urban entertainment magazine on college campuses, *Mad Rhythms*, which reached more than four million students. In addition she has written articles for such respected publications as *Black Enterprise, Upscale, Impact,* and the *Electronic Urban Report*.

She has authored the nonfiction work *The Blueprint for My Girls: Life Lessons for Young Women* and the novel *Exclusive* and is working on *The Blueprint for My Girls in Love*. Her work has been recognized by national magazines, radio, and television.

The Signals Agency is Shiraz's own marketing and management firm that handles entertainment clients and the booking of tours and speaking engagements.

For more information on Yasmin Shiraz, please visit: www.yasminshiraz.net.

What are you experiencing? Use this space to free your mind, free your thoughts, develop your soul. Write, write, write.

LaVergne, TN USA
16 February 2010
173202LV00003B/1/P